Donald Hall

in conversation with

Ian Hamilton

Donald Hall

in conversation with

Ian Hamilton

B
T
L

First publishd in 2000 by

Betwe en Th e Lines

9 Woodstock Road
London N4 3ET
UK

Tel: +44 (0)20 7272 8719
Fax: +44 (0)20 8374 5736

E-mail: betweenthelines@lineone.net
Website: http//www.interviews-with-poets.com

ISBN 0-9532841-4-X

Jacket design: Philip Hoy

Printed and bound by

Biddles Ltd
Unit 26
Rollesby Road
Hardwick Industrial Estate
King's Lynn
Norfolk PE30 4LS
UK

Between The Lines

Between The Lines publishes more than usually wide-ranging and more than usually deep-going interviews with some of today's most accomplished poets.

Some would deny that any useful purpose is served by putting questions to a writer which are not answered by that writer's books. For them, what Yeats called 'the bundle of accident and incoherence that sits down to breakfast' is best left alone, not asked to interrupt its cornflakes, or to set aside its morning paper, while someone with a tape recorder inquires about its life, habits and attitudes.

If we do not share this view, it is not because we endorse Sainte-Beuve's dictum, *tel arbre, tel fruit* — *as the tree, so the fruit* — but because we understand what Geoffrey Braithwaite was getting at when the author of *Flaubert's Parrot* had him say:

> 'But if you love a writer, if you depend upon the drip-feed of
> his intelligence, if you want to pursue him and find him —
> despite edicts to the contrary — then it's impossible to know
> too much.'

Volumes 1-4, featuring W.D. Snodgrass, Michael Hamburger, Anthony Thwaite, and Anthony Hecht, respectively, are already available; others now being prepared will feature Thom Gunn, Seamus Heaney, Richard Wilbur, Paul Muldoon, Donald Justice and Hans Magnus Enzensberger. (Further details are given overleaf.)

As well as the interview, each volume will contain a sketch of the poet's life and career, a comprehensive bibliography, archival information, and a representative selection of quotations from the poet's critics and reviewers. It is hoped that the results will be of interest to the lay reader and specialist alike.

– Other volumes from BTL –

W.D. Snodgrass
in conversation with Philip Hoy
ISBN 0-9532841-0-7

Michael Hamburger
in conversation with Peter Dale
ISBN 0-9532841-1-5

Anthony Thwaite
in conversation with Peter Dale and Ian Hamilton
ISBN 0-9532841-2-3

Anthony Hecht
in conversation with Philip Hoy

ISBN 0-9532841-3-1

– Forthcoming –

Thom Gunn
in conversation with James Campbell
ISBN 1-903291-00-3

Richard Wilbur
in conversation with Peter Dale
ISBN 0-9532841-5-8

Seamus Heaney
in conversation with Karl Miller
ISBN 0-9532841-7-4

Paul Muldoon
in conversation with Lavinia Greenlaw
ISBN 0-9532841-8-2

Donald Justice
in conversation with Philip Hoy
ISBN 0-9532841-9-0

Hans Magnus Enzensberger
in conversation with Michael Hulse and John Kinsella
ISBN 0-9532841-6-6

Contents

Donald Hall

photograph courtesy of
Linden Frederick

©

A Note on Donald Hall

Donald Hall was born in New Haven, Connecticut, in 1928, the only child of Donald Andrew Hall (a businessman) and his wife Lucy (née Wells). He was educated at Phillips Exeter, New Hampshire, and at the Universities of Harvard, Oxford and Stanford.

Hall began writing even before reaching his teens, beginning with poems and short stories, and then moving on to novels and dramatic verse. He recalls the powerful influence on his youthful imagination of Edgar Allan Poe: 'I wanted to be mad, addicted, obsessed, haunted and cursed. I wanted to have deep eyes that burned like coals – profoundly melancholic, profoundly *attractive*.'

Hall continued to write throughout his prep school years at Exeter Phillips, and, while still only sixteen years old, attended the Bread Loaf Writers' Conference, where he made his first acquaintance with the poet Robert Frost. That same year, he published his first work.

While an undergraduate at Harvard, Hall served on the editorial board of *The Harvard Advocate*, and got to know a number of people who, like him, were poised for significant things in the literary world, amongst them John Ashbery, Robert Bly, Kenneth Koch, Frank O'Hara, and Adrienne Rich.

After leaving Harvard, Hall went to Oxford for two years, to study for the B.Litt. While there, he found time not only to edit *The Fantasy Poets* – in which capacity, he published first volumes by two more people who were set to make their mark on the literary world, Thom Gunn and Geoffrey Hill – but also to maintain four other valuable positions, as editor of the Oxford Poetry Society's journal, as literary editor of *Isis*, as editor of *New Poems*, and as poetry editor of *The Paris Review*. At the end of his first Oxford year, Hall also won the university's prestigious Newdigate Prize, awarded for his long poem, 'Exile'.

On returning to the United States, Hall went to Stanford, where he spent one year as a Creative Writing Fellow, studying under the poet-critic, Yvor Winters. In *Their Ancient Glittering Eyes* – a book which merits comparison with Hazlitt's 'My First Acquaintance with Poets' – he recalls Winters greeting him with the words, 'You come from Harvard, where they think I'm lower than the carpet,' adding, after a pause, 'Do you realize that you will be ridiculed, the rest of your life, for having studied a year with me?'

Following his year at Stanford, Hall went back to Harvard, where he spent three years in the Society of Fellows. During that time, he put together his first book, *Exiles and Marriages*, and with Robert Pack and

9

Louis Simpson also edited an anthology which was to make a significant impression on both sides of the Atlantic, *The New Poets of England and America*.

Hall was appointed to the faculty in the University of Michigan at Ann Arbor in 1957, and apart from two one-year breaks in England continued to teach there until 1975, when, after three years of marriage to his second wife, the poet Jane Kenyon, he abandoned the security of his academic career, and went with her to live in rural New Hampshire, on the farm settled by his maternal great-grandfather over one hundred years earlier.

Ever since that time, Hall has supported himself by writing. When not working on poems, he has turned his hand to reviews, criticism, textbooks, sports journalism, memoirs, biographies, children's stories, and plays. He has also devoted a lot of time to editing: between 1983 and 1996 he oversaw publication of more than sixty titles for the University of Michigan Press alone. At one time, Hall estimated that he was publishing a minimum of one item per week, and four books a year.

In 1989, when Hall was sixty-one, it was discovered that he had colon cancer. Surgery followed, but by 1992 the cancer had metastasized to his liver. After another operation, and chemotherapy, he went into remission, though he was told that he only had a one-in-three chance of surviving the next five years. Then, early in 1994, when the thought uppermost in his and his wife's minds was that his own cancer might reappear, it was discovered that she had leukaemia. Her illness, her death fifteen months later, and Hall's struggle to come to terms with these things, were the subject of his most recent book, *Without*.

Winters's prediction that Hall would never live down the year he spent studying in California could hardly have been more wrong. Forty-five years after leaving Stanford, Hall is one of America's leading men of letters, the author of no less than fourteen books of poetry and twenty-two books of prose. He was for five years Poet Laureate of his home state, New Hampshire (1984-89), and can list among the many other honours and awards to have come his way: the Lamont Poetry Prize (1955), the Edna St Vincent Millay Award (1956), two Guggenheim Fellowships (1963-64, 1972-73), inclusion on the Horn Book Honour List (1986), the Sarah Josepha Hale Award (1983), the Lenore Marshall Award (1987), the National Book Critics Circle Award for Poetry (1988), the NBCC Award (1989), the *Los Angeles Times* Book Prize in poetry (1989), and the Frost Medal (1990). He has been nominated for the National Book Award on three separate occasions (1956, 1979 and 1993).

A Note on Ian Hamilton

Ian Hamilton was born in 1938, and educated at Darlington Grammar School and Keble College, Oxford. He co-founded and edited *The Review* (1962-1972), and *The New Review* (1974-1979), and was for several years poetry and fiction editor for the *Times Literary Supplement* (1965-1973).

His verse publications include: *The Visit* (Faber, London,1970), *Fifty Poems* (Faber, London, 1988), *Steps* (Cargo Press, 1997), and *Sixty Poems* (Faber, London, 1999). His prose publications include: *A Poetry Chronicle: Essays and Reviews* (Faber, London 1973/Barnes and Noble, NY, 1973), *The Little Magazines: A Study of Six Editors* (Weidenfeld, London, 1976), *Robert Lowell: A Biography* (Random House, NY, 1982/ Faber, London, 1983), *In Search of J.D. Salinger* (Heinemann, London, 1988/Random House, NY, 1988), *Writers in Hollywood, 1915-1951* (Heinemann, London, 1990/Harper, NY, 1990), *Keepers of the Flame* (Hutchinson, London, 1992), *The Faber Book of Soccer* (Faber, London, 1992), *Gazza Agonistes* (Granta/Penguin, London, 1994), *Walking Possession* (Bloomsbury, London, 1994), *A Gift Imprisoned: The Poetic Life of Matthew Arnold* (Bloomsbury, London, 1998), *The Trouble with Money and Other Essays* (Bloomsbury, London, 1998), and *Anthony Thwaite in Conversation with Peter Dale and Ian Hamilton* (BTL, London, 1999).

Hamilton has also edited a large number of books, amongst them: *The Poetry of War, 1939-45* (Alan Ross, London,1965), *Alun Lewis: Selected Poetry and Prose* (Allen and Unwin, London, 1966), *The Modern Poet: Essays from 'The Review'* (Macdonald, London,1968/Horizon, NY, 1969), *Eight Poets* (Poetry Book Society, London, 1968), *Robert Frost: Selected Poems* (Penguin, London, 1973), *Poems Since 1900: an Anthology of British and American Verse in the Twentieth Century* (with Colin Falck) (Macdonald and Jane's, London, 1975), *Yorkshire and Verse* (Secker and Warburg, London, 1984), *The 'New Review' Anthology* (Heinemann, London, 1985), *Soho Square (2)* (Bloomsbury, London, 1989), the *Oxford Companion to 20th Century Poetry* (OUP, Oxford, 1996), and *the Penguin Book of Twentieth-Century Essays* (Penguin, London, 1999).

Between 1984 and 1987 Hamilton presented BBC TV's *Bookmark* programme. He now serves on the editorial board of *The London Review of Books*.

A Conversation with Donald Hall

In November of 1998, Donald Hall flew to Ireland, to give readings in Belfast and Dublin. Before returning to the United States, he stopped off for a weekend in London, specifically for the purpose of being interviewed by BTL. The interview was recorded in North London, and to the edited transcript subsequently prepared have been added a number of supplementary questions and answers.

Sorry to do this to you again. I read of your saying somewhere that you had done over two hundred interviews.

I must have; if you count ones written up by reporters. Three hundred? I've decided not to do any more in the States because there is so much repetition in these things. But this one is mainly for Britain, isn't it? I want to do this one.

Yes, well, we think of you as someone who was influential on poetry in the English scene. And then you disappeared. We lost track of you.

And I to some extent lost track of you, I suppose, though I do subscribe to several British magazines: *Agenda*, *PNR*, the *TLS* and the *LRB*.

You must be more up with it than I am.

I made many friends in my two years at Oxford. And I came back twice for a year afterward. You probably remember, I lived in the little village of Thaxted, and went up to London to make my living on the BBC, 1959-60, and 1963-64. Long ago. I used to go to those Wednesday noontime gatherings of poets at the Salisbury, St Martins Lane. I can't remember if you were ever there. One time Graham Greene came in, had a glass, went out again. Nobody spoke. Ted Hughes came on occasion, Alvarez.

When were you at Oxford?

1951-53

So were you here for the Festival of Britain?

I arrived that summer of 1951, probably August. Yes, I went to parts of the Festival. I remember seeing real Henry Moores out in the open for the first time. Battersea Park? I didn't know him at that stage. Not until 1959-60, a Thaxted year, when I was given a journalistic assignment to interview him.

For The New Yorker?

No, that was later, in 1963.

Well, I'll come back to Moore later on. Right now, for England, I think we need a bit of background about your childhood, upbringing. Your father seems to have had less literary influence on you than your grandfather. You seem to have divided your childhood between them.

I grew up in suburban Connecticut, on a block where the houses were identical, the cars identical, and the educations. Then I would take the train from New Haven to Boston, up to the village – well, hardly a village: the depot at West Andover. My grandfather would be waiting there with the horse and buggy to take me back. My grandparents never had an automobile. As opposed to the suburbs, there were enormous differences, house to house – oh, income, age, education. If there were, say, a retarded child, the child would come to church like everyone else. He wouldn't be stuck away in an institution somewhere. People weren't put off by the unusual or eccentric. Very early in life, I chose the country over the suburbs, the old culture over the new. It's also true that I chose my mother's place rather than my father's. I was an only child, a mother's boy. And my mother read me poems when I was a child, mostly from an anthology called *Silver Pennies*.

The grandfather then was your mother's father?

Yes. He was a great reciter of poetry, I mean recitation pieces like 'Casey at the Bat'. While he was milking his Holsteins by hand – it was an old-fashioned mixed farm, no longer viable today, very little cash – he would recite poems. I would sit on a stool beside him.

So he was milking rhythmically, metrically?

Yes. It was old-fashioned oratory. He would set back his head and intone: 'Mighty Casey ... has struck out!' Poor old cow.

Now I know why you like those lines of Richard Wilbur's ...

Oh, that wonderful couplet:

> We milk the cow of the world, and as we do,
> We whisper in her ear, 'You are not true.'

Yes, I chose the country over the packed suburbs, and the older people

14

instead of people my age. I was a split child – more suburban in terms of time, of course.

But one location must have represented school and one holiday.

Absolutely. Olson and Eliot both chose Gloucester, the summer place where they didn't go to school. You see it again and again; the summer place represents freedom and laziness as opposed to the discipline of school. When I went to Harvard I didn't have a car but I borrowed Robert Bly's and drove up to see my grandparents, which was the anti-Harvard device of the young Harvarder. Finally, in 1975, I moved back to this place, encouraged by my second wife, Jane. I feared that, in the spirit of the fox and the grapes, I would find it sour, that the country culture would have been sunk under the television culture. Not so. Although it is true that many farms were gone, my cousins worked perhaps eight hours a day in a factory, or caretaking the houses of summer people, and then went home and tended an enormous garden, raised a pig and chickens. But I'm not thinking only of farming; the rural culture is attitudes, ways, stories. When I was a child, my grandfather would tell stories and when people came calling they too would tell stories. I listened to the old people telling stories to each other. I came back thirty years later and there they were – middle-aged people turned old, doing the talking and telling these stories to each other.

And you chose not the farming but the stories.

The stories, the landscape.

As a child, did you ever think of becoming a farmer?

I didn't think of myself becoming a farmer. There were many men who lived alone in shacks and scraped a life together. I remember reading the Sears Roebuck catalogue and thinking of myself as a hermit in the woods. There's a story in *String Too Short to be Saved* about a cousin of mine who lived like that, 'A Hundred Thousand Straightened Nails'. The woods were full of these people. When I moved back, Wendell Berry wrote me – we are close now but we didn't know each other so well then – and he said, 'Don, don't put in too many acres at once.' And I wrote back, 'Don't worry about a thing.' There's a curious resemblance between what I do and what my grandfather did. My grandfather made his living by the garden, by milk, by slaughtering some animals, shearing sheep, trading eggs for salt and coffee. I have made my living out of writing articles for magazines, doing children's books, textbooks, poetry readings. My work is various, many compartments, as his was.

15

Was this all slightly unfair on your father?

Yes. He was a sad man who was not doing what he wanted to do. He was the only child of a self-made man. His father had gone through fifth grade, then had worked hard and built up a business delivering pasteurized milk to suburban doorsteps. Milk again, the suburban end and the country end. After college, my father taught at a prep school, Cushing Academy, for two years, and loved it, but he wanted to marry my mother and he was making $1000 a year. In 1927 you didn't get married until you could support your wife. She was a schoolteacher with the same salary in New Hampshire but you could not be a married woman and a schoolteacher then. So he went to work for his father in the dairy business, in order to make enough money to marry, and he was miserable; he hated working for his father, who was hard on him, the eldest child of the self-made man. He could never do anything right. He would come home weeping from the office. Someone had slighted him, someone had crossed him.

This weeping you refer to, one gets this picture of him practically weeping all the time.

No, but the weeping was important to me. Men didn't weep in the suburbs. The fact that he wept was a gift to me, although he was ashamed of weeping.

A gift?

Yes. He would allow feelings to show at a time when men were not supposed to show feelings. He tended to weep and rush out of the room. I grew up extremely conscious of his unhappiness in his work. He came home to his lunch one Saturday and shook his fist over my crib and said, 'He'll do what he wants to do.'

Who told you that story?

My father and my mother both told me that: 'He'll do what he wants to do.' When it turned out to be poetry, maybe they swallowed hard a couple of times, but they were kind. When I went to Breadloaf I was sixteen; it was what I wanted to do.

That's the Breadloaf Writers' Conference, run by Middlebury College?

Yes. My parents paid for me to go. $100 for two weeks, I think. My father was only making $60 a week.

16

You have referred to your background as rather bookish.

There's irony in that. My parents belonged to the Book of the Month Club and read *The Reader's Digest*. When I was sixteen I thought this made them wretched bourgeois consumers. Later I realized that at least my parents *did* read books; not everybody's parents read books. After supper, one sat in one's chair reading a book. My father read Kenneth Roberts, a historical novelist, popular then, who wrote decent prose. My father was a snob about prose. He didn't read the *Reader's Digest* much; he knew the difference between good and bad prose. My mother would read on the one hand Thoreau and on the other Agatha Christie, and didn't seem to care about the difference. But, mostly, he was a negative example for me. I saw him unfairly and cruelly as a man who had been bullied into doing things he didn't want to do. I was not going to be like that.

But what about the grandfather's side to this? He recited, so you say. There were no books?

He read, and it was bad stuff: Kathleen Norris; Zane Grey; Joe Lincoln, a comic novelist of Cape Cod. He read the same books over and over again. My grandmother did not read but he did, every night. She had taken Latin and Greek at High School, and then taught school, but she didn't even read the newspaper. She sat sewing, mumbling to herself, as he was reading the same book for perhaps the twentieth time, giggling. It was another example of reading, though not a literary example.

My grandfather was doing what he wanted to do. Sometimes his work was painful, like getting ice out of the pond in February or chopping wood in January. Winter was painful. (For me it is beautiful; I don't have to do anything outdoors.) My grandfather loved the improvised day: you don't know quite what you will be doing; you know you will work all day, but not exactly on what, or when. If the sun shines, hay; if it's drizzling, something else. As I said, I compare his work to my life as a freelancer: at the desk all day but not sure what sort of writing I'll be doing, in what order or when. I love the freedom of improvisation, whim almost. What is important is that I keep working.

When did you begin to see yourself as a poet?

Very early on, twelve or thirteen. What's unusual is that I never changed my mind. I decided for sure at fourteen that that's what I was going to do.

You met this guy, didn't you, who said, 'I am a poet'?

When I was fourteen I went to boy scout meetings now and then. I never got beyond tenderfoot. I went to get out of the house. When I was a freshman in High School, he and I met each other at a scout meeting. He was sixteen, I was fourteen. 1942. We were bragging to each other, and I said I had written a poem in study hall that morning, and he said, 'You write poems?' I replied, 'Yes, do you?' And he drew himself up and said, 'It is my profession.' Remember the old film, *Bonnie and Clyde*, when Clyde says, 'We rob banks'? That's what his answer sounded like, or 'I am a pirate.' It was romantic and anti-bourgeois. I loved the notion, at fourteen, of wearing a cape and having deep eyes that burn like coals.

That was your idea then of the poet?

Sure.

Did you say you met this professional poet again later?

Yes, 1956. I was walking down Michigan Avenue in Chicago where I went to do a reading. That's how I remember the date. I looked into a breakfast place and there he was. That guy looks like Dave Johnstone, I thought, and I walked in, and yes, it was Dave Johnstone. He came to my reading, and later sent me a volume of poems – sorry, a manuscript. My recollection is that it was not up to much. I wrote him and I think that's the last we heard of each other.

I bet it was.

Well, we had a pleasant breakfast.

Did you find out whether he now had a 'real' profession, so to speak?

He was doing marriage counselling.

How interesting. So that's what happens to poets who aren't up to much.

If he's alive now, he's seventy-two. He was important to me then. How does one come upon what one does for the rest of one's life? When I was twelve I had discovered Edgar Allan Poe, coming to him by way of horror movies. That was when I began to write poems. And stories.

But you got on to modern poetry very early.

At fourteen, through Dave Johnstone. In New Haven, Connecticut. He knew eighteen-year-old freshmen at Yale who read T. S. Eliot. So I bought the *Collected Poems* of Eliot, such as was available in 1942, a blue cloth volume which I still have. I read it through and annotated it, misspelling nearly every word. Beside 'I will show you fear in a handful of dust' I wrote: 'epegramatic simbolism'. And in our high school literature anthology there were poems by H.D., which were good for a fourteen-year-old – the early imagistic poems, with good sound, a Greeky sweetness of sound. And dance-like. I imitated them. She was the first modern poet I learned anything from. Then I read Eliot, and I heard that there was a man who worked for an insurance company forty miles north who was a published poet. I read Wallace Stevens and ricocheted rapidly from poet to poet. I found Hart Crane, whom I adored.

This was Untermeyer's anthology?

Louis Untermeyer was the editor of the textbook I read in high school, where I found H.D. Later I discovered the famous anthologies. There was one that he published, maybe '43 or '44, *A Treasury of Great Poems*, in which he wrote little biographies, romanticized and inaccurate, for every poet. I discovered that Hart Crane had jumped off a boat when he was thirty-one, which of course attracted me. I was fickle, spending two months in love with one poet, then another. Of course I was going to school, learning from these poets, but not on purpose.

Were you thought to be a bit weird by your schoolmates?

Oh, sure. At high school I was totally weird; at prep school, I was a bit weird. It was: 'Hey, fruit poet.'

Like fruit bat.

It wasn't until I went to Harvard that people stopped saying 'Fruit poet.'

Was this because of your cloak, do you think?

Yes, the internal cloak. I think I enjoyed – forgive the word – the *alienation*.

You probably would have, yes. Did it help with the girls?

I loved the girls.

Yes, but did they love you?

Some of them, yes. A year ago this month I was in Nebraska for eight days, mostly reading at Indian reservations. I went into a high school in a tiny town called Niobrara, which had probably never entertained a poet before. The teacher, talking somewhat nervously of this double class, said that perhaps I should begin by talking about how I got started when I was their age. I told them about Dave Johnstone. A boy in the front row raised his hand and said, 'Did you do it to pick up chicks?' And I said, 'Yes. My god, how could I have forgotten?' The fact that I was a terrible athlete helped me go in this direction, hoping to interest the girls.

I had the idea that you were a pretty good athlete?

No, terrible.

But you write about sport.

I love baseball but I couldn't play it. I worked on poems and wore the cloak thinking it would make me interesting to girls. The cheerleaders were not remotely interested, but there were the girls who wanted to be actresses.

Oh, the neurotic, suicidal girls.

With them, it had some effect.

Good. But a bit awkward, though.

I couldn't claim great erotic success.

Then you were sent to Exeter.

Yes.

Which was connected to Harvard?

It's what we call a prep school, and in my time it was an avenue to Harvard.

But you were born in New Haven, where Yale is?

I grew up assuming I would go to Yale. My parents had gone to a small college called Bates, which is quite good, but my parents had greater ambitions for me. Yale was where I was intended to go. If I had gone to Yale – this was just after the War – I would have had to live in my parents' house. But the real reason I chose Harvard was that the Exeter teachers I admired had all gone there. I remember thinking about the University of Chicago, which was good, but the Exeter teachers, especially one who was important to me, had gone to Harvard. Along with most of my class, I went to Harvard.

Wasn't there a teacher at Exeter who told you to stop writing such drivel?

Yes. He was important, because he made me angry and stubborn.

You showed him poems? And he'd say, 'Take this away, it's drivel'?

He was teaching the special third-year English class, the brightest kids, and I asked to be admitted to his class. He said that he had read my poems in the Exeter literary magazine and that they were terrible. Did I still want to come into his class? Of course I took the challenge, and I said Yes. After two or three themes he had assigned, he gave us a free theme: you could do anything you wanted. I told him that I wanted to do poems. He said, 'I told you what I thought of your poems but if you want to ...' Well, I gave him some. It was the middle of the winter term, my first year. I had *Es* in a couple of subjects, flunking Latin, Mathematics, possibly History. He announced, to a whole class of students who had straight *As*, that I was flunking. (Normally we never knew each other's grades.) He added that I was flunking because I was spending all my time writing this junk. He spent the entire period reading my lines aloud and making sarcastic comments. To begin with, the class of cruel adolescents laughed. Then they stopped, became silent. I never said a word, but sat there angry and wounded. When class was over, some of these boys, for the most part usually sarcastic, touched me on the shoulder. They were appalled. I went back to my room and howled tears of anger. I decided I would spend more and more of my time working on poems. Not so many years later, in 1955, I published *Exiles and Marriages*. Probably it was 1956 when Exeter asked me to come back and read. In the English department room, there was this guy who had grumbled about me when I was his student. The other teachers did not know about my humiliation, and they thought it was amusing to ask him to introduce me. I had the opportunity to take revenge but I didn't do it. Later I took unconscious revenge, the kind you permit yourself. I wrote a piece for the *New York Times Book Review*, a little essay in which I proved – a deconstructionist before my time – that Wordsworth's daffodil poem was actually about money, investing in the visible, then living off the investment in daydreams. At the end I said if anyone thought his or her appreciation of the poem was troubled by my revelation, he or she didn't care about the poem in the first place, just about a postcard of daffodils

21

from the Lake District. A few days later I had an envelope from Exeter and inside was a postcard of daffodils from the Lake District and a message from my old teacher saying, 'I suppose your fingerprints are still on it.' I have no recollection of him passing that card round the class.

Can we name this man for posterity?

A marvellous name: Chilson Hathaway Leonard.

Glad you hated him.

But his opposition was useful.

But there was a counterbalancing influence, wasn't there?

There was. He wasn't a teacher of mine, but he lived in my dorm. I would stop him on his rounds, and we would talk about Gerard Manley Hopkins.

What was his name?

Leonard Stevens, who adored modern poetry. He was the only one. It was wartime and the teachers were mostly older men. There was a general consensus in the English department that Pound, Eliot, Stevens, and Cummings were all frauds. Robert Frost was the great American poet and his heir apparent was Stephen Vincent Benét.

You had already met Frost, of course. Was that at Exeter?

At Breadloaf, between my first two years at Exeter, when I was sixteen. Because my eighth grade English teacher – who was a fool – liked Frost, and because the teachers I didn't care for at Exeter liked him, I tended to think that he couldn't have been good.

You changed your mind, though?

Frost was and is a marvellous poet.

Tell us something about Breadloaf.

I suppose that Breadloaf was the first of the writers' conferences, which have proliferated at an alarming rate. There must be hundreds now, all over the United States, meeting for a weekend perhaps, a week, two weeks. I'm not sure quite how Breadloaf got started. I think Frost took some of the credit for it, which is strange because he was such a loner himself. Theodore Morrison was director, when I was there. His wife was Katherine, Frost's lover and assistant. People could attend either as auditors or as contributors. Auditors sat around and listened, lectures and workshops and readings. Contributors submitted their manuscripts, which were worked over in public; and they had at least one conference with a teacher, someone who ran workshops. My conference was with Louis Untermeyer, believe it or not. When my things were discussed in a workshop, Frost was not there. I wonder if this were not contrived, because of my tender age. Frost had a way of being nasty at these workshops. I got nothing in particular out of the criticism my work received there – I brought short stories, a novel or part of a novel, and many poems – but it was good to meet Frost, to hang around grown-ups who were writers.

Did you show Leonard Stevens your poems?

Yes, and he encouraged my endeavour. He didn't tell me I was a good poet but he was delighted to have a student who liked modern poetry and could talk about it, and who tried to write it. I asked him if we could meet in the evening to talk about poetry or Plato or whatever. We started with Plato and moved on to Yeats. We spent hours discussing poetry outside the classroom. My third book, A *Roof of Tiger Lilies,* is dedicated to Leonard and his wife Mary.

How old were you then?

I turned seventeen at the beginning of my second year.

You went to Exeter at the age of?

I turned sixteen a few days after I arrived.

And Harvard at?

Nineteen. I lost a year because I was ill. I went to Exeter for the third year of high school, only one more year to do, but half way through my first senior year I became ill.

There's something I didn't understand. Somewhere you say that you were at boy scout camp – well, you were somewhere anyway – and that your father got a postcard saying you had been taken ill. Then you talk about an Oedipal angle ... What was this about?

23

It was after Breadloaf. The following January at Exeter I became ill. In retrospect, it seems psychogenetic, but no one thought of referring me to a psychiatrist then. I had at least the hint of a migraine headache every day, some days all day, and a low temperature too. No one ever found a cause for these symptoms. Finally, a doctor said to throw away the ther-mometer. I got better. While I was ill, my father got a postcard from someone who had been at Breadloaf the year before, saying that he really ought to have a heart to heart talk with his son. It was the end of the War when I was at Breadloaf, V.J. Day happened while I was there, and I had done nothing but talk about poetry and chase women. There were almost no men there. A couple of gay guys. A couple of elderly men. I mean: slightly younger than you now – much younger than me. Women were short of men. I ran after one after another. Three dates a day. I read them poems. I think I know the woman who wrote that card. Well, my father worried that I might have had a venereal disease.

And did you?

No, no, I didn't.

So this anonymous card arrived, and by then were you actually ill?

Yes.

But you think this illness might have been psychosomatic?

I can think of two other writers who were fond of their mothers – James Wright and John Fowles – each of whom had a disease in the mid-teens that allowed them to go home and be taken care of by their mothers. After that year I was ready to fly from the nest, but I couldn't have ear-lier, I guess. That's where the Oedipal element might come in.

So you went home?

I went home and was taken care of, went to the hospital for a while for observation. They wondered about a brain tumour because of the head-aches. With the primitive medicine of the time there wasn't much they could tell. Obviously I didn't have a brain tumour. I went back to Exeter to do the senior year again and by this time it was after the War and there were veterans there, older people, and I had a much better time. I was a year older than my other classmates, classes had become easy. I was no longer flunking. I got into Harvard.

We'll come to your Harvard years in a few minutes. Can we first go back

24

a bit to Breadloaf, and the meeting with Frost? You've written about this but not everybody here would know. What was that like?

Probably by that time I loved twenty of his poems, after dumping him earlier because the idiots liked him. I've come to love seventy-five or eighty. At sixteen it was enormously exciting to meet him. I remember the first time I saw his visage. There was an opening night lecture in a room that had French doors all along one side. Frost was outside. The land sloped so I saw his head first and then the rest of his body as he was rising toward the lecture room. I was thrilled.

Later, he read *The Masque of Mercy*, which was not very good, and afterwards a fatuous woman introduced me to him, telling him that I was an excellent young poet. I was embarrassed. Frost was perfunctory. Later, for an hour or two, I sat on the porch with Frost and some other people and listened as he talked. He asked me where I was going to go for college and I said Harvard. He said how he'd been there. He was always competitive with every male, even a sixteen-year-old when he was in his sixties and famous. He said he didn't really need Harvard, perhaps I did. One time, not long before he died, he came to Ann Arbor. I remember walking through a building of classrooms with him and I said idly, 'That's a room where I teach.' Frost had been poet in residence, way back, and he said, 'They didn't make *me* teach.' That's the sort of thing you could expect. I didn't resent it. I couldn't be in competition with a man born in 1874. But he never let up. Knowing him over the years, I admired his stubbornness. Those early years of neglect remained with him forever – the years when he wrote poems and no one accepted them; old neglect was an engine that powered this energy, this vanity. Meeting him and knowing him at Breadloaf, when I was sixteen, was inspiriting, in that this poet was a real man, a human being. I saw him being foolish; I heard him say amusing things, witty things.

Did you think of Frost at that time as being old-fashioned?

Not really. But it was a period when you weren't supposed to admire Eliot and Thomas Hardy at the same time. Another terrible teacher had a holograph Hardy poem on the wall, as a result of which I never read Hardy's poems until I was thirty. Now, he has become one of my favourite poets in the language. I saved him till my thirties, because of the silly business that you're not permitted to like contemporaries who appear to be in opposing camps. I did manage to like Frost. Inconsistent of me.

Now let us come to Harvard.

Because of the illness I told you about I was a year later going there than

25

I might have been, which was good, because in class I sat beside people who had been captains in Italy three years earlier.

How did you find it at Harvard? Who were your contemporaries?

I was on *The Harvard Advocate,* with Robert Bly, John Ashbery, Kenneth Koch.

A fair line-up, an anthology-full. Did the Advocate *poets hang out together?*

Yes, and I dated Adrienne Rich. Robert Bly had a blonde girlfriend, and we'd sit as a foursome drinking beer. Adrienne and I did not become friends at that time, but later. A few years ago I met the fourth person, not a poet, pretty and bright. I asked her what we talked about those nights. She said, 'Well, you and Robert and Adrienne would say your poems.' She was our audience. Yes, it was an extraordinary line-up. Creeley had gone down just the term before I came up; he had overlapped with some of the others. I met him in the Grolier Bookstore. I think Creeley got married and went to live in Littleton, New Hampshire. He went to New Hampshire to farm chickens and was probably about as good a chicken-farmer as Frost. I knew Frank O'Hara well. He was not on the *Advocate,* but in my first year I took a creative writing-course, taught by John Ciardi, who was a good teacher and a promising young poet then. He'd been in the Pacific, must have been in his late twenties. O'Hara I met in that class. Up front were these two guys: O'Hara and his room-mate Edmund St John Gorey, the illustrator, as he was to be. Gorey never spoke, but O'Hara was enormously funny, witty, concise. I'd never seen anything like *that* before. He was probably only two years older than me but he'd been four years in the navy. Adrienne Rich could not be on the *Advocate* because she was female, but we published her. Bly had found her at a jolly-up – an informal dance at Radcliffe for the boys and girls to meet each other – and he came back saying [puts on the voice], 'Met this girl from Baltimore, father's a surgeon, knows all about modern poetry.'

Who was thought to be – if anybody was – the star, the leading light in the Advocate *crowd?*

Ashbery.

Really? What was Bly like in those days?

Extraordinarily skinny. He wore three-piece suits and striped ties.

I always think of him as wearing Mexican blankets, for some reason.

That was later. A year after we met, he was into checked shirts. I thought he had changed but in fact he had reverted. He had been trying to be a Harvard man for a few months. He'd just arrived from St Olaf's. He grew up in a small town where his father was a farmer. He'd walked to school barefoot, he told me. He went from Madison High School to the navy and then to St Olaf's, largely Norwegian in its origins, and transferred to Harvard as a sophomore. When he was first there, he had felt rather assaulted by Harvard. He had hung Picasso Blue Period on his walls and his room-mates had ridiculed him.

Did you see him as a poet then?

At first I saw him as a critic. He was an unsmiling brown-suited presence who had the Harvard manner of that time: denigration. 'Have you ever seen a performance of Shakespeare that you liked?' – he was quoting someone, I think – 'Actually, not.' The two things everybody said, about everybody else, were: 'He's rather bright,' or 'He's not very bright.' It was a little like the Oxford manner.

Very familiar, yes.

Bly was a critic and he wrote short stories. Finally he showed me the poems he was working on, and, as I remember, the first that I saw were very much like Robert Lowell's *Lord Weary's Castle,* which had just come out and was powerful.1947, 1948.

And it had an impact there and then?

Before I came up, in an issue of the *Advocate* there was a long article, a dialogue among students arguing over Lord *Weary's Castle.* It was front-page news. Wilbur came out with *The Beautiful Changes* then, and for a long time people spoke of 'Wilbur and Lowell'. Sometimes, 'Wilbur and Lowell and Roethke'. Roethke was born in '08; Lowell in '17; Wilbur, '21. Roethke was coming on the scene with *The Lost Son. Lord Weary* was Bly's favourite and together with *The Beautiful Changes* it was mine. On the *Advocate* we divided between those who looked back to Yeats and those who looked back to Auden. Ashbery, O'Hara, and Koch were Auden men: Bly and I were Yeats. Adrienne was eclectic. On the *Advocate,* we didn't all like each other, but it was good; we argued poetry all the time. Bly and I were close. O'Hara was in another group, but we were friends for quite a while. Ashbery and I were friends, not close, but I enjoyed talking with him. I still do.

I read somewhere that before you joined the Advocate *they accepted a poem of yours, and that Koch told you this wouldn't have happened had he been present at the editorial meeting where it was okayed. Was that candour or abrasiveness? What manner of man was he, is he?*

Actually it happened after I became an editor. Koch did not attend the editorial meeting at which the *Advocate* accepted my first poem. I met him on the street the next day and told him, cheerfully, that the editors had picked a piece of mine. He said, more or less, 'It wouldn't have happened if I had been there.' He was abrasive, I suppose candid. Arrogant.

Do you know my story about Ashbery writing a poem for the *Advocate*? We were pasting up an issue and there was a blank half-page. We said, 'John, we need a poem, we haven't had you for two issues. You *know* you've got a poem.' He said, 'No, no.' 'Oh come on, John, you know you've got something.' 'Well, maybe.' He went back to his dorm and came back with a poem.

Twenty minutes later, I suppose? I think I remember the story.

The first line was 'Fortunate Alphonse, the shy homosexual' – I can't remember the rest. About five years ago I told him this story and asked him if he remembered it. He said, 'I took longer then.'

So he confessed.

I wasn't there but I was told that he was at a lecture by Seamus Heaney, a few years ago, and Heaney was speaking like Pound of the cleansing effect of poetry on language. John said, 'Mine gives it a blue rinse.'

Was there gay solidarity in those days?

People were remarkably out of the closet in the Harvard of '47-8-9. Then came McCarthy, the UnAmerican Activities Committee, the Korean War, the collapse of the left – and people went back in the closet. When I was first there I was startled to see men holding hands as they walked around. Mind you, if they got outside Harvard into Cambridge they were liable to get beaten up. At the *Advocate* it seemed clear who was and who wasn't gay. I remember one candidate being interviewed. He was hopeless, and at the end of our negative vote John said, 'But he was attractive.' He was making a joke that acknowledged his sexuality. O'Hara once – he gave wonderful parties, and he drank a lot – I remember joshing him and comparing him to Oscar Wilde. Frank turned to me, in his way, and said, 'Oh, *you're* the type that would sue.'

Things must have changed by the time you arrived, because I remember reading in David Lehman's book about the New York School that after Koch got onto the editorial board of the Advocate, *he tried to get Ashbery onto it as well, and encountered a problem. Evidently, the magazine had been short of funds, and though someone had been found who was prepared to bail them out, this was only on condition that Jews, homosexuals and alcoholics wouldn't be allowed to serve on the board. Quite how Koch, a Jew, got past this, wasn't made clear, but, according to Lehman, Ashbery was keeping his homosexuality a secret in those days, and Koch, not knowing any different, protested that Ashbery was straight and threatened to resign if the appointment didn't go through – which it did, of course.*

At some point during the war, the *Advocate* closed down. I heard rumours that the trustees had decided that it was a gay club. And an important trustee was a notable anti-Semite. Perhaps the trustees' overseeing was tardy and distant. I never heard the story about Ashbery, but it doesn't surprise me.

Did the composition of the board owe anything to the influence of Auden? Lehman says that Auden delivered the University's Phi Beta Kappa poem, written specially for the occasion, in 1946, and adds that '[t]he chain of friendships that turned into the New York School began the year Auden read these lines at Harvard Yard.'

I never heard this story. I did not come up until the autumn of 1947.

Did Auden show up while you were there?

No. I never saw him there. Poets came by: Stephen Spender in my first term as freshman. I wasn't a great admirer of his work but the excitement was extraordinary – seeing on the platform a man you'd read since you were twelve or thirteen. William Carlos Williams came. Dylan Thomas. Eliot came and read. The *Advocate* would generally give a tea for the visiting poet. The tea consisted of pitchers of martinis, possibly beer, but most visitors were subjected to martinis. When I took Dylan to the party from the lecture hall, he said to F. O. Matthieson, 'Will there be something to drink at this party?' Matthieson said, 'The boys will have martinis but there will be beer.' Dylan said, 'Oh, no, no, I've done my work; now I can get down to the serious stuff. Scotch will do for me.' We sent out and got some.

You took against him, pretty much?

Dylan? Oh, he was awful that day. He was cruel.

You've written about him staring down some girl's dress, embarrassing her ...

The girl *was* embarrassed, and she was intended to be. But I knew him later, in sober circumstances, and stayed up talking poetry with him.

In Remembering Poets *you recall putting out a special issue of the* Advocate, *reprinting Eliot's contributions in time for his sixtieth birthday. The magazine was still in financial difficulties, and someone thought a birthday issue for Eliot might bring in some much-needed cash. Discovering that you were left with a blank page, it was agreed that it should bear the dedication, 'For the Sixtieth Birthday of T.S. Eliot'. Unfortunately, a slip-up occurred, and when the issue came back from the printers the dedication was found to read, 'For the Sixteenth Birthday of T.S. Eliot.' You blame the Emersonian self-reliance of the printer, saying that he assumed that Eliot was a fellow undergraduate and couldn't believe he might be that long in the tooth. But to come to my question: you decline to name the editor who'd had responsibility for this issue, and I wonder why. It was Robert Bly, of course, who later took full responsibility, saying that he'd not proofed the issue properly, but I wondered why you kept his identity a secret?*

I wanted to let Bly say it himself. I'm not sure that the poems were proofed at all. I remember Bly assigning two of the editors to type out the Eliot poems from bound copies of old issues. Everybody was drunk, including the typists.

There's an amusing letter from Wallace Stevens, sent to you in June of 1950, when you were putting together The Harvard Advocate *anthology. You'd sent him the things you wanted to include, and he wrote back as follows: 'If you use the things which you enclosed with your letter of June 20ᵗʰ, I shall have to go out and drown myself. This is especially true as to the poems. Have a heart. Of the two prose pieces I remember the first, but not the second – yet I suppose that I wrote the second. Definitely: no.' You did meet Stevens, I know. Was he as down-to-earth as the tone of that letter suggests?*

The letter from Stevens that I remember included a memorable phrase: 'Some of one's early things give one the creeps.' I did meet him one time, when he came to the Signet (more or less a literary lunch club) for brunch just before a Harvard/Yale game, I think in 1950. Because we had corresponded, I approached him. He was standing beside a friend, maybe somebody from the office, and he was embarrassed to meet an admirer of his poems. He shifted on his feet, and we exchanged a few sentences. I remember him saying 'shit' and 'fuck', which surprised me. The following Monday Eliot was coming to town to do a reading, and there would be an *Advocate* party. Martinis. So I asked Stevens if he could stay over, and it would become a party for both of them. He said, 'No, no, I have to get back to the office.'

When you went from Harvard to Oxford, who were the English gods with whom you hoped to make contact? I suppose there was Eliot.

I'd met Eliot at Harvard and he asked me to come around and see him at Faber. He was very kind.

What was your general grasp of the English scene? Did you have any?

I felt that the Americans were better. I came with that attitude. I remember years later at the Salisbury a poet from Seattle, whose name I forget, said, 'There are more poets in Seattle than there are in England.' This was a tone of the time. Later, Alvarez's anthology, *The New Poetry,* suggested that the Americans were better than the English, yet there was English condescension in this general judgement: the Americans are better because they are raw, young, bumptious, whereas we are an old, sophisticated, decadent nation, smarter but without the energy.

But in '51 at Oxford there must have been deep prejudice against Americans.

I think that 'deep prejudice' is too much to say. There was condescension, more from the dons than from the other students. There was of course the automatic one-upmanship, in which my nationality could be used against me. I did not suffer, because I felt superior. In the condescension – I need to emphasize – there was always a whiff of inferiority.

In my second Oxford year, I wrote a long two-part piece called 'American Poetry since the War' for *The World Review.* I was drawing particular attention to Lowell, Wilbur, and Roethke. It was badly written. I didn't know a damn thing about writing prose then, but they did publish it. It helped to bring new American poets to England. For a long time I wanted to bring English poets to Americans and American poets to the English. You won't ... Oh yes, I bet you do remember this: for many years, later, I did an annual round-up for the Third Programme on the year's American poetry, picking six new books and talking about them.

We all remember it.

This was part of my ambassadorship business.

So you were already a power figure?

I suppose I was. At Oxford, I was a little older than the others.

But how did that happen? There you were, this American, arriving in Oxford with your Lowells and your Wilburs, whom nobody had ever heard of ...

The naiveté of the current Oxford poets startled me. I remember one of them telling me that one must *never* use a contemporary reference in a poem, because the poem would become dated. I quoted him Chaucer about the meat pie, the Jack of Dover ... In general they seemed to know very little about what Americans tended to call 'technique'. They were all in favour of sincerity. I enjoyed pointing out what I considered incompetence. I also wore plimsolls and khakis, and I gathered that this dress was intimidating. Once, Christopher Ricks, whom I did not know at Oxford, told me I'd been quoted as saying: 'Ya gotta fake it, but ya gotta fake it good.'

So your first impressions weren't very positive?

When I first arrived I was appalled. Everybody was so rude. In Christ Church, if I asked someone to pass the salt they'd manage to insult me passing it. But this was just the Eton, public-school thing, the dance of the mating turkeys. If you insulted them back when they insulted you, then you could begin to be friends.

Was it anything to do with your being a Yank?

My nationality and my accent were used against me, but anything else would do. I later learned that being a Yank could be very useful. You could get away with things that ordinary Englishmen in the House were not allowed to do. People would write my gaffes off as ignorant American slips. In the House you didn't put yourself forward in the university at large, joining OUDS or *Isis*. If you did, you were on the out. I could get away with it because I didn't know any better.

There's a funny poem in A Roof of Tiger Lilies, *'Christ Church Meadows', in which the speaker, an American studying in Oxford, gets horribly upset when mistaken for an Englishman by a fellow national, a tourist:*

Here too I saw my countrymen at large,
  Expending Kodachrome upon a barge.
From chauffeured Car, or touring Omnibus,
  They leered at me, calling me 'them', not 'us'.
A jutting woman came to me and said,
  'Your Highness, can those big white geese be fed?'
'Yankee go home,' I snarled. 'Of course the Swans,
  As the Bard puts it, are reserved for Dons.'
She fainted then, beside two Christ Church porters,
  Who cast her, as I told them, on the waters.

Hell, I don't think the American 'gets horribly upset'. I do think it's funny that the American, mistaken for English, immediately adopts a nasty British persona: 'Yankee go home ...' You recognize the limerick that I alluded to? I'm sure you do. I remember the woman that I thought of, but she said nothing like what I have her say. A busload of Americans wandered through the House. I was walking along in my tweeds and gown, when an old lady, struggling along at the end of the line, looked at me and said, 'Well, I don't see the brains oozing out.'

It's difficult to say who comes off worse, the English or the Yanks. Why did you go to Christ Church in the first place?

I was put there. I had a Henry Fellowship and the Dean of Christ Church at that time was a Canadian who had been a Henry Fellow. He grabbed as many Henry Fellows as he could. I didn't know one Oxford college from another. I was glad, eventually, to have been in the House because it was one of the most unAmerican colleges. It wasn't intellectual, of course; it was full of Wykehamists, Harrovians, Etonians. It was a strange and alien world to me. Tony Thwaite came up the second year; Alastair Elliott was a friend writing poetry. There were only eight Americans out of five hundred students. In Balliol there were seventy-five Americans, more or less, and they tended to stay together, rather proud of their national background. At the beginning I felt utterly alien. Then, by November, I sent some poems to *Isis*. I never heard from them and in the next issue there were two poems of mine. I started getting invitations to parties because I had published poems.

Very strange.

It seemed at that time that publishing poems was a social asset. Not in the House but outside. Because I was older I could be amused by it. I remember the first literary party I was asked to. I had recently fallen down in Tom Quad – I had a migraine which affected my balance – and my scout had given me a cane because I was stiff in the right leg. I took this cane to the party, sat in a corner with my leg up.

Irresistible.

A young woman came up to me and said – forgive my English accent – 'Do you need that cane or is it pure affectation?' By that stage, I knew that this question need not be unfriendly. Two months earlier I would have been devastated. It wasn't that at Harvard everybody was kind to each other, but I knew the language and manner of its put-downs. Soon I began to know the language of Oxford.

You started a magazine, didn't you?

Oh, yes. At one point I was editing four things while I was at Oxford. Outside, I was poetry editor of *The Paris Review*. At Oxford I edited the Poetry Society's mimeographed journal, and I started *New Poems*. I did The Fantasy Poets for a while. Then I was literary editor of *Isis*. John Bowen, who was editor of the whole magazine in my third term, asked me to be editor the next autumn. I hesitated, because I realized that I was to be married that September, and I couldn't come back to do a B. Litt and edit *Isis*. I agreed to be literary editor instead.

You married your first wife. Was she someone you had known from before?

Yes, from Radcliffe College. We lived out on the Banbury Road in my second year. I was in Meadow Buildings the first. I did my B. Litt. on eighteenth century prosodists – 'with especial attention to Edward Bysshe and Joshua Steele.' Catherine Ing was my supervisor because nobody else at Oxford gave a damn about prosody.

Did you finish it?

Yes. It was no good, but I got the B.Litt. I used to work in Duke Humphreys Library, very cold, but so old and beautiful. I came up to the B.M. to see some books that were not in the Bodleian. I was interested in the sound of poetry. The sound was first for me; without sound there was no poetry. My obsession narrowed for a while to metrics because that was how I wrote at that stage. When I was elected to the Society of Fellows at Harvard my project was to write a prosody of twentieth century poetry.

So there were these four periodicals? The Fantasy Poets involvement, how did that happen?

It was not my doing. Oscar Mellor, the printer-publisher, approached the Poetry Society. The President before me would have been Michael Shanks. You knew him?

The name, but not him.

He chose the first four Fantasy Press pamphlets. I was fourth. Elizabeth Jennings was first, James Price ...

What became of James Price?

He became an editor at Penguin. Last I heard, he had a small press, but I haven't heard from him for some time now. He denies it, but he was, in fact, a talented young man, much influenced by John Crowe Ransom. Later I took over the series.

With Oscar Mellor ...

Did you know Mellor?

Yes. I edited a little magazine that he printed. I actually lodged for a time in his house. I never worked out how interested in poetry he really was.

I think he was interested in drinking coffee with the poets at that little pub between the theatres, off Gloucester Green as it then was. Oh, he was a *flâneur* and charming.

How old was he then?

He must have been in his thirties. I never thought that Oscar permitted himself opinions about poetry.

No, he would smile and stroke his beard and that was about all.

His wife, Iris, worked hard for him. When I got the Newdigate Prize, the poem had in the past always been published by Blackwell. But I said, 'No, the Fantasy Press is going to do it.' I had a condescending letter from Basil Blackwell, making it clear *he* knew how to behave. Oscar printed it.

Under your stewardship, the Fantasy Press published pamphlets by quite a few people, three or four of whom went on to establish themselves as serious writers.

The one I was proudest of was Geoffrey Hill's.

How did you meet Hill? Through the Poetry Society?

It was because he published a poem, May or June of '52, in *Isis*. It was the first time I came upon his name. A poem called 'For Isaac Rosenberg', I think. It began, 'Princes dying with damp curls ...' The poetry editor of *Isis* thought it was an ironic reference to the death of the king.

In 1952.

Yes. At the House, we wore black armbands because we were a royal foundation. I had a Poetry Society party in my room and invited Hill because I admired his poem. When I first talked with him, Geoffrey was more or less scraping his feet and tipping his cap. I thought he was mocking me. Of course he wasn't. From Bromsgrove, Worcs., and all that, he had hardly met a literary type, least of all an American. I said to him then that I was taking over the editorship of the Fantasy Poets and would he submit a manuscript? He seemed pleased to be asked. I went back to the United States that summer to get married, and he sent a manuscript, forwarded to me up in New Hampshire. I read 'Genesis' and 'Holy Thursday', and 'God's Little Mountain'. I could not believe it. You can imagine reading these poems suddenly in 1952. I read them and I was amazed. I remember waking up in the night, putting on the light and reading them again. Of course I published them.

That was the Fantasy Press's 11ᵗʰ book, and, what, the third under your editorship? You and Hill became good friends?

In my second year, Geoffrey and I became close. In '53 he turned twenty-one and I drove him to Bromsgrove to visit his parents.

When you first went to Oxford, who were the names to you?

I was bringing American poetry to Elizabeth Jennings, Alastair Elliot. Geoffrey Hill had read an Oscar Williams anthology.

Oh, Oscar Williams was everywhere in those days, wasn't he?

I remember Geoffrey asking me what Richard Eberhart was like. Well, I knew Eberhart from Cambridge. Geoffrey had the notion that Eberhart walked through the streets at night wearing a dark cloak with deep burning eyes – the old cloak, the old burning eyes. I told him that Dick was short and pudgy and sweet. I remember talking about Lowell with Geoffrey. I might have introduced him to Lowell's poems. I'd brought them with me.

Is it true that shortly before your departure for the States, Hill was so upset that he actually laid into you, landed a few punches?

That's a bit of an exaggeration. When my first wife and I were about to go home, Geoffrey was desolate, angry that we were leaving him. One night we went out to a pub – Geoffrey, my wife and I, and three visiting young Americans. The Trout. Some of us had too many pints. Geoffrey and I went outside and he hit me – tapped me rather lightly, actually – five or six times on the face. The last time it smarted, and I hit him back – probably harder. It was raining, and Geoffrey marched off into the night, back toward Oxford. I gathered the rest of us together, in the car, and drove down the road and found Geoffrey marching along in the rain, with his raincoat over his shoulder. I persuaded him to get back into the car. We returned to the apartment and after a while Geoffrey began saying lines of poetry. I thought he was improvising. I believe it was a poem, never collected, that he had been working on. 'An Ark on the Flood', maybe.

Another of the people you published while working for the Fantasy Press was Thom Gunn.

That's right. I believe I also got *Fighting Terms* for the press, outside the series.

But he was Cambridge.

Before the end of my first year, John Lehman had a magazine of the air on the BBC Third Programme called 'New Soundings' and we would all listen to it at Oxford. All of a sudden there was Thom Gunn. We noticed! Daniel Ellsberg – who later came to note with *The Pentagon Papers* – was a friend from Harvard and invited me to Cambridge.

Don't tell me Ellsberg wrote poetry.

No, no. When I was over there, I looked up Thom Gunn. We talked and got to know each other. He introduced me to Karl Miller.

There was that little blue book, Poems from Cambridge, *that Karl ed-*

37

ited. Gunn was in it and I think Hughes.

I didn't know Hughes at that time. I got Thom to come over to Oxford and he spent a long weekend in our flat. We had a party for him and the Oxford poets met the Cambridge poet. The next year, when I was studying with Yvor Winters at Stanford, Thom wanted to come to the United States.

Yvor Winters invited him?

I told Thom about the fellowship, he applied, and Winters chose him. Thus Thom became a citizen of San Francisco. That's his country. He and I read there together, last January. He once wrote a letter to the *TLS*, after George MacBeth had said something in praise of syllabics, saying that I was the one from whom he had learnt syllabics.

He went further in his review of The One Day, *calling you 'the inventor of syllabics in our time.'*

Of course, Elizabeth Daryush, Marianne Moore, and Auden had done syllabics earlier.

You were the first American to win the Newdigate Prize?

No, *Time* magazine printed an article saying I was the first but somebody wrote in saying that others had won it earlier.

The subject was 'Exile'?

The year before it had been 'Captain Carlson'. He was the man who almost went down with his ship. C. Day Lewis, naturally, chose that topic – he was Professor of Poetry at the time. In my year it was 'Exile' and since from about the age of thirteen I had cultivated alienation, and I was now in a foreign country for the first time, the subject was made for me. I was hardly an exile, though.

The poem had to be quite long, didn't it?

I thought it had to be about three hundred lines. It *had* been the previous year. I had never written a poem longer than forty-eight lines.

You stretched something?

I stretched myself and wrote a poem of a hundred and twenty lines, with

38

a two-line refrain. Before I published it I got rid of the refrain. In the end, it was a hundred lines. Yes, I was thrilled to win the Newdigate.

Did it have to be a very formal poem?

The announcement – I have told Americans this forever and ever – said, 'This poem need not be written in heroic couplets.' Isn't that amazing? It was 1952. I trust it doesn't say so any more. As I wrote it, each stanza had two iambic quatrains separated by a couplet of ten syllables and six syllables. I think the couplets were the best part. George Barker read it and wrote me a letter, saying, 'Ah, my dear Samuel Hall. What a nacreous nostalgia! What a yearn of pearls!'

Al Alvarez was a contemporary at Oxford, I believe?

I knew him. There was a time, a brief time, when George Steiner, Al Alvarez, and I were a little troika.

How sweet!

We would wander around Oxford together saying, 'These people don't love literature.'

So Al was an Oxford figure?.

Definitely, with The Critical Society.

Yes, of course. Al started that, didn't he?

I don't remember. It was a combination of American New Criticism and Leavis. My second year at Oxford, Steiner (whom I had known at Harvard and the year earlier in Oxford) came up from London and called on me. He had, I think, a desk at *The Economist*. After supper there was a knock on the door and it was Geoffrey Hill. George and I quarrelled – what about, I don't remember – and in his pique he intimated that I was collecting acolytes and that Hill was one of them. That made the break with George.

Did you quarrel with Al?

Yes. I don't want to publish how or why. It would be self-serving.

But that's what these interviews are for. Who would you say was the star Oxford poet in the early 1950s?

Elizabeth Jennings was the star when I came there. Geoffrey was the best poet. He was writing intensely – at nineteen years of age.

Were people like Larkin impinging in the way that Lowell had at Harvard?

This was before Larkin, as it were. Larkin was still published by the Fortune Press. He was not yet a figure.

The Less Deceived *was 1954.*

I went down in 1953. I don't recall that we knew him. Can't remember discussing him. I think he may have been on John Wain's successor to Lehmann's 'New Soundings' radio magazine.

The older figure then, I suppose, was Auden?

Yes, but he was in America. Poets visited the Poetry Society all the time. Louis MacNeice, Dylan Thomas.

Robert Graves?

No, not in my time. I met him later in Ann Arbor in my first year there. W. R. Rodgers came.

Martin Seymour-Smith, was he a contemporary?

No, he and a poet whose name I forget – Michell Raper? – went down a term before I got there. Their names were bandied about, but Elizabeth Jennings was the older star. She had gone down but was still living in Oxford and was very much part of the scene.

And then came Stanford.

I was admitted to Harvard Graduate School to do a Ph.D., because I had decided that I'd make a living by teaching at college. It was not automatic at that time. I didn't really want to go to Graduate School. Pearce Young was an American poet – yes, a Fantasy Poet – who'd had a Stanford Fellowship and told me about it. I applied, looking for a way to avoid Graduate School.

It was called the Winters Fellowship, wasn't it?

No. It was, I think, the Stanford Creative Writing Fellowship. Obviously if you went there to do poetry you worked with Winters.

Though not everyone who went there did work with him, did they? Wendell Berry and Robert Hass, for example.

If you went to Stanford on a poetry fellowship, you worked with Winters, and he required that you attend one of his literature classes each term. I think that Wendell was at Stanford to write prose. Robert Hass was doing a regular Ph.D.

I had read Winters extensively, *In Defence of Reason*, but I loved Yeats, whom Winters loathed. Of course, there was his relationship with Hart Crane, although he finally turned against Crane.

I didn't know of the connection.

Crane stayed with Winters in California. They had corresponded – Winters and Crane and Tate all corresponded. (Once, Tate and Winters had a quarrel and Tate set out from Tennessee with a pair of duelling pistols and a couple of bottles of bourbon. The bourbon ran out in Texas and he turned around and went back. Probably that's apocryphal but that's the story Winters told me.) I applied for the Stanford Fellowship, and didn't hear anything. I applied for a Fulbright as well and was turned down. I felt resigned to Graduate School. Then a letter came from Stanford, and I spent the year in California. I found out later that Janet Lewis, Winters's wife, and a man who was head of the department, had persuaded Winters to take me. I drove across the country to Stanford with my pregnant wife in a Morris Minor. We arrived exhausted and the phone rang. It was Winters, saying, 'Do you have enough money?' He was attentive to the needs of his students, one of the things which was father-son. (When he gave Thom Gunn the Fellowship, Winters called me and said, 'He won't be able to drive, can't afford a car. Will he ride a bicycle? I have a bicycle.') After asking me if I had money, he said, 'Come over to my place; I'll cook you a steak.' The great American thing. We walked into the house and he said two things within the first five minutes: 'You come from Harvard. That's where they think I'm lower than the carpet. You realize that you will be ridiculed for the rest of your life because you spent a year studying with me?' I came to like him and I learned a tremendous amount about literature; he was a learned man and a good teacher.

You never became one of the elect, though, did you? Like J. V. Cunningham.

Oh, no, no. By the way, Cunningham and Winters quarrelled a lot. Cunningham was an offshoot, not a disciple.

41

Who were his favourites?

Edgar Bowers. Robert Pinsky. There was a man named Edward Field. The most slavish of his imitators were no good. Some survived and prevailed – Bowers, Gunn and Pinsky, for instance. I learned about prosody from Winters – and I had been studying it for more than ten years. I learned a lot about the seventeenth century, although I'd already read a good bit. He went into Barnabe Googe and Fulke Greville. He gave a course called 'The Theory and the Practice of the Criticism of Poetry' – which should have been called 'The Systematic Destruction of the Collected Works of Gerard Manley Hopkins and W. B. Yeats'. About Hopkins I didn't know enough, but I knew a lot about Yeats, so I sat there while he destroyed Hopkins, but then it came to Yeats. Every time he finished demolishing a poem he would turn to me and say, 'Mr Hall?' And I would defend the poem. Thereupon – he was a wonderful arguer, talking for victory – he would slice through my argument, leaving it chopped on the floor. I still believed what I believed, but it was fine to argue with him – or try to. Stimulating.

About Hart Crane: Winters championed him at first, but denounced 'The Bridge', and that was the end of the friendship. But let me tell you: We had a three-hour workshop in the afternoon. I always arrived early in order to talk with him. I could make him laugh. One time I came in and he was sitting reading Hart Crane and I said, 'Why are you reading Hart Crane?' I asked because Winters's dismissal had been so hard. He looked up. 'Because it is so beautiful,' he said.

Just before I left Stanford, he had a party at his house. He handed me the ice bucket and said, 'Would you get me some more ice, son?' *Son.* I melted, and I thought then: it's time to get out of here.

Well, if he'd said, 'Boy!'

It was affectionate, fatherly affectionate. I left. That was when I took the Junior Fellowship at Harvard for three years.

Your memories of Winters and those recorded by Gunn in The Occasions of Poetry *are very similar, aren't they? Even down to the brutally dismissive letters he eventually sent, yours received after publication of* Exiles and Marriages *('It went on and on, with much anger and much punitive rhetoric, with accusations of literary and moral fault'), Gunn's after he'd mailed him a group of poems ('he wrote back that they were simply journalistic and maybe I should try to learn how to write prose instead').*

Gunn worked for a couple of years with Winters. I did one year, and that was enough. I learnt a tremendous amount from him but it would have been difficult to stay. You were with him or against him.

What is this Society of Fellows at Harvard?

It was founded by a President of Harvard, who had a private fortune, in 1933, I think – to allow young scholars of promise to avoid the Ph.D. Or it was to be a substitute. In general, it didn't work out that way, but I used it that way. Early on, Harry Levin never did graduate work. He and B.F. Skinner were elected two terms in a row. Six years.

But why would someone invent something to avoid the Ph.D?

Lowell – the President I just mentioned – felt that American education was becoming dominated by the Ph.D, and that Ph.Ds were too German. I've not read his argument. The fellowship was often for people who were combining things that could not easily be combined in a gradu-ate program. There's a story of someone coming to Harvard saying he didn't know quite what to do his Ph.D in. He liked mathematics, par-ticularly partial differential equations, but he was also into Sanskrit and musicology. 'You're a Junior Fellow,' he was told. All Souls and the fellowship at Trinity, Cambridge, were models for the Society.

So you could just hang about for three years doing what you liked?

Yes, no formal study. No teaching. Three years suffering the burden of freedom. It drove some people crazy, but many found it marvellous. Richard Wilbur had been a junior fellow, the first poet, and John Hol-lander and I were elected the same year; and Paul de Man – 1954-57.

Was it well endowed?

At that time the salary was something like $4,000. It increased over the three years.

It must have been something everybody wanted to do.

You had to be nominated by someone. Archibald MacLeish nominated me. Harry Levin had been my tutor, junior and senior year, and he was a senior fellow.

How did you know MacLeish?

I took one of his courses. He became Boylston Professor, in, what, 1949?

43

He taught English for the first time, creative writing and a large lecture course in poetry. When he put me up for the Society, in 1954, I was flown across country from Stanford to Harvard to be interviewed.

Did you live in Cambridge? You had children by then.

One child, born at Stanford. Winters actually wrote an epigram on a child so fortunate as to be born in California. He always teased me about New England. He said, 'Oh, I know that New England countryside, all that flat land with rivers running through it. I spent a whole summer in Gambier, Ohio.' We would laugh. The epigram is now lost. The Junior Fellowship was a time of intense intellectual competition and excitement. When I was twenty-five years old I introduced two Nobel Laureates to each other, one a physicist and one a chemist. 'Mr Eliot' came once a year. Edmund Wilson came twice a year. The most intelligent fellows and visitors were the mathematicians and the logicians.

When did these meetings take place, at dinner?

Yes. Imitation high table. A little pretentious. Port and Madeira, cigars.

And some grand person to sit next to?

Usually, there were four or five visitors. I ate beside Nabokov one evening. Many times I talked with physicists. I didn't understand what they were talking about but I loved to hear their language. I'd hear remarks like, 'The meson particle problem won't break; it'll just sag,' a physicist's joke. The first dinner, I sat next to a saturnine young man and asked, 'What do you do?' He said, 'Mathematical linguistics.' I said, 'I've never heard of it.' He was Noam Chomsky. Marvin Minsky was another member.

Three years is a long time. Were you writing poems?

Mainly. Reading a tremendous amount. Working on things. I lived in Cambridge a year and a half. Then moved to Lexington to a little ranch.

Your first book, Exiles and Marriages, *which came out in '55, made quite a splash, with good reviews in* Time, The New York Herald Tribune *and the* New York Times, *a nomination for the National Book Award, and, most important of all, perhaps, the Lamont Prize. All of this must have been very gratifying? Did you take it in your stride, or did it all come as a bit of a surprise?*

I'm afraid I took it all in my stride. After all, why *shouldn't* my work receive such honours? Ha! It was not much of a book. Too long, too much inferior work. It was surprising that it got so much attention, but I think that *Time* – and other journals – were *looking* for somebody new to come along. Lightning struck on me. (I didn't know anybody who was responsible for these prizes or nominations.) Later, I paid my dues for having been overpraised. When *Remembering Poets* came out in 1978, the same year as *Kicking the Leaves*, two reviewers of the prose book said that it was poignant to read about Hall's youth, because he was once a promising poet himself. That's how much my reputation had sunk.

There were harsh words about the book from one influential critic. Randall Jarrell was at his most wounding in a piece he did for The Yale Review: *'The worst poems, perhaps, are those that confirm us in our own commonplaceness ... Donald Hall's poems are very commonplace, but they are so complacent about themselves that they shock us into aware-ness of their commonplaceness.' Do you remember that notice, and, if so, how you felt about it?*

Actually, Jarrell's comments did not bother me. I had put him down in a long article I wrote about current American poetry. I never liked his poems. I loathed 'The Death of the Ball Turret Gunner'. I think I was tickled, as if he wrote out of hurt feelings. A couple of other reviews – by Stanley Kunitz and William Arrowsmith – bothered me much more. Each was partly positive, but each pointed out faults that were genuine. And shameful. Their criticism had me walking up and down.

All the writers I know can recite you the worst lines ever written about them in reviews. Memorized. Can tell you every anthology from which they were omitted. How much energy does one give to this bitterness? I know too many poets who have wasted their lives and energies in bitter-ness over what did or did not happen, and their poetic reputations. Eve-rybody is ambitious. It's a total waste to sit down at the desk thinking about slights, hurts. Better to try to make a poem.

A new Dunciad *is maybe needed. Everybody in it.*

It would be so long.

You spoke earlier about being Poetry Editor of The Paris Review? *How did that come about?*

I knew George Plimpton at Harvard. He was at Cambridge while I was at Oxford. He and his friends in Paris were starting a new magazine, but they didn't have a poetry editor. George came over from Cambridge to play tennis for Kings, and after the match he and I had dinner and some drinks. At that time he asked me to gather poems – first he himself gathered the Newdigate poem – for the first issue. Between the first and the second issue I was asked to be Poetry Editor.

How long did you continue?

Until the first year I was in Thaxted, 1959-60. I resigned in irritation as the quarterly was appearing about one and a half times a year. Constantly, I kept poets waiting two years for publication. I did enjoy my time on it. I was avaricious to find the best poets of my generation. Of course I was not always right, but I solicited W.D. Snodgrass, James Wright, Louis Simpson. I wanted to be like a baseball scout. I published Geoffrey Hill, Thom Gunn, Robert Bly, W.S. Merwin, Adrienne Rich.

What about the interviews you did for The Paris Review, *with Eliot, Moore and Pound? Am I right in thinking that you'd already resigned as Poetry Editor by the time you did the first of those?*

I had already resigned as Poetry Editor, but George Plimpton has kept my name on the masthead as editor ever since. It was natural that he would turn to me when the interviews expanded to include poets. I'm not sure whether he suggested Eliot. Eliot was obvious, of course. George might have suggested Pound first. As I remember, I had scheduled an interview with Pound when Pound was still at St. Elizabeth's, and Pound cancelled it, saying that *The Paris Review* was evidently part of the pinko-usury fringe. When I met him in Rome he was sane.

That interview with Eliot was the first interview with a poet The Paris Review *ever commissioned.*

Yes.

Apart from Eliot and his wife, two other people were present when that interview was done, as you explain in Their Ancient Glittering Eyes: *'The day before, I came to New York to visit Robert and Carol Bly; the night before the interview, Louis and Dorothy Simpson came to dinner. Neither Simpson nor Bly had met Eliot; both admired him; both wanted to make his acquaintance. Thus I arrived at Mrs Cohn's apartment, the next morning, equipped not only with a deck of questions on three-by-five cards, not only with a cumbersome reel-to-reel tape recorder, but with two tape technicians.' But Bly tells the story slightly differently, as I'm sure you know: 'The days before I had said: "Don, let me go with you." He said, "No, Robert." "Come on Don. He'll be dead before so long. I'll never get to see him if you don't take me along." "No, Robert. You never behave yourself, you'll say something wrong." Louis was with us and he said, "Come on, Don, take me along too, come on, it's not fair." Don said, "No, I'm not taking either one of you along. Robert never behaves himself, and I'm going by myself." We really complained, we cussed him out. But something fell through. The next day he came by and said, "Robert, may I use your tape recorder?" "Aha! Both Louis and me ..." "All right, all right, I'll take you both along; you and Louis will be tape recorder technicians; I'll introduce you both as tape recorder technicians." So that's the way it happened. We were glad to go.'*

My recollection is entirely different. I think the *Review* supplied the tape recorder. Robert likes to characterize me as saying things like 'Robert never behaves himself...' It would have been 'Bob' at the time, for heaven's sake. Sometimes he makes himself the naughty child and I the strict mother.

When did The New Poets of England and America *come out – the Hall, Pack and Simpson anthology, as it's better known?*

1957.

So you were doing that when you were at the Society of Fellows?

Yes, it came out before I left the Society in 1957. Pack had a contract for an anthology and then felt diffident and asked Simpson, and Simpson persuaded him to add me. The three of us often voted two to one.

We don't know much about Robert Pack.

Robert Pack was a leading young poet for a time and then taught at Middlebury College. He ran Breadloaf for years. As a young man he was funny and energetic. I didn't mind working with him, but our tastes clashed. When a further selection came out, I did the English poets alone and he did the Americans. Simpson wanted out. I didn't want to work with Pack, one on one, because we differed so much. In the Penguin *Contemporary American Poetry* I had my own say, and I was relatively ecumenical, even in the first edition. The Penguin had an effect on things, chiefly because it was a Penguin, selling many copies in Australia, New Zealand, India, Belfast. It brought American poetry to the attention of people in the Commonwealth. Maybe a hundred thousand copies.

It was some time before Al's The New Poetry, *which was when – 1962?*

47

My anthology came out in 1962. I cannot remember when Al's did. In all, I was proud of it.

The New Poets of England and America. *I used to carry that book around. It was my introduction to these poets. Snodgrass, for example. And, indeed, to one or two English poets. It was a book that was very much there. More than the Penguin, for me.*

The Penguin was old news in England, but not elsewhere. Twenty years later, though, where are The New Poets of England and America?

Well, yes, in some cases. But that's true with all these things.

Where is – où sont – Melvin Walker La Follette?

But were there people you now wish you had included?

Yes. Originally, we included Ashbery, whom I knew and liked. Louis was not so keen but acceded to my persistence. When the manuscript was submitted, it was fifty pages too long, and because Louis wasn't all that keen on Ashbery, and Pack couldn't stand him, Ashbery was excluded. Therefore he was in the counter anthology, Donald Allen's. If we had printed him, Allen would not have done so.

But that did have an effect. For example, I had never heard of Ashbery in the late 1950s. Twenty, thirty years later he seems to be in a different sort of ambience from yours. I think of him almost as a different generation. Had he been in your anthology and not the Allen, I would perhaps have had a somewhat different perspective on him.

I wish he had been. It wasn't until after that book came out that I heard the name of Allen Ginsberg. *Howl* was 1956. Louis had been at Columbia with him, but he hadn't seen the new work. If we *had* heard of him, I don't think we would have included him. I knew of Creeley, but the only Creeley I had read was early pseudo-Cummings stuff, and I decided that he was no good. Later, I saw those early pamphlets and became very enthusiastic about him.

But Creeley was thought of as Black Mountain. That didn't get much of a showing, did it?

No, not at that time, no. I had not read the good stuff. I had talked to Creeley for four hours about poetry when I met him in Cambridge in 1950 or so. Then I read the Cummings stuff in disappointment. He was in Spain later, into Charles Olson. I knew Black Mountain was around, but we were writing in rhyme and metre; we all pretended, at least, that we loved Williams. I certainly loved him. I praised the first *Paterson*, highly, in a review I did when I was an undergraduate. When the bifurcation took place, it was a swift thing. The war of the anthologies, as it was called, may have been useful – but soon we set about coming together.

Who was or is Donald Allen?

He was an editor in New York, a friend of poetry. He was on the lookout for poets. When I started to publish in England, he had his ear to the ground. When I came home, he had a party in New York to introduce me to poets.

But what was he? A publisher?

An editor.

Of what?

He was working on *New World Writing* then, I think. He'd worked for other publishers as well. Grove? Later, when he lived in San Francisco, he turned up as the editor of *The New American Poetry, 1945-1960*.

Which was conceived as a retaliation against yours. He said that, didn't he?

It was perfectly true. We were an orthodoxy of the moment, while these other strands were developing. We were the academy, the enemy. But, only two or three years later, in 1960, Denise Levertov got me to review the first Maximus poems in *The Nation*. There was an effort on both sides to get connected. I met Snyder and began to read the real Creeley. Most of us pursued ecumenical projects – but not at first. When I first saw *Howl* I hated it. It was an attack on my citadel.

I may be wrong but it seems that at that time there was more combative squabbling in America between schools, poets, and then everybody in the end agreed to be rather chummy. Everything became a bit bland as each side saw some merit in the other, and nobody wanted to rock the boat.

It's also true that most of The New Poets of England and America, who continue to survive, are people who changed course. James Wright, Louis

49

Simpson, Bly, Merwin.

You could not have predicted 'The Deep Image' school, so-called, from reading James Wright's first book.

The Green Wall, which was in the Yale Younger Poet series. The second also, *St Judas*.

Yes. They were in that Wesleyan University Press series, weren't they?

I was an editor there. I got Bly, Simpson, and Wright there. Dickey. And we published Ashbery. The crazy *Tennis Court Oath*.

When did Bly, Wright and Co. begin to loosen up?

When I was at Oxford I remember, the year I was living in the House, Bly sent me a bunch of Shakespearean sonnets, and before I could get around to responding, he wrote a letter, saying, 'Don't read them, they're too old-fashioned.' He'd begun to see the light.

Yes, but what was this 'deep image'?

Bly never used that phrase. And neither did Wright. That was Jerome Rothenberg and Robert Kelly. It's become a tag that's stuck to Bly. It's not particularly important.

But the magazine, The Fifties, *used to speak about it all the time.*

Bly talked about 'the image', mysteriously. I think it's more or less the symbol. *The Fifties* was influential and funny, combative. In its way, it was ecumenical. The first essay, every issue, was about one or another contemporary American poet. In the first issue it was Creeley. Bly wrote that essay. They were always signed 'Crunk', and one was written by James Wright. The rest were by Bly.

But whatever it was that distinguished that school came about via The Fifties *and then* The Sixties *magazine. I became aware of it in the early to mid '60s. Surrealism and South America and all that. You touched on it in your introduction to the Penguin.*

Bly spent a year in Norway from 1956 to 1957. His forebears were Norwegian and he took a Fulbright wanting to see where his family came from. There, he discovered an international modernism as opposed to an English language modernism. If it was surrealist, it was not Breton. I would call it expressionist distortion, more like Trakl and the Spaniards. Nothing like this had been tried in America. Bly discovered it and promoted it. And Wright admired Trakl earlier. That's the way they fit together. Translation and the promotion of Latin-American poetry were at the centre of what was positive in *The Fifties* and *The Sixties*. What was negative was almost as important. Do you remember he gave the award of the Blue Toad to Brooks and Warren, and to John Hollander? There were the literary jokes, like Edward Pygge.

Oh, I think Edward learnt a lot from those magazines. – There was a poet in them I liked called St Giraud.

Oh, that was Bill Knott. He's still around.

Why St Giraud?

I don't remember why he called himself that. Once he published a book called *Posthumous Poems*. He's stayed Bill Knott since those days.

The Dark Houses, your second collection, appeared in 1958, and was reviewed very favourably by a number of people, including Anthony Hecht, who wrote: 'Donald Hall's first book was the Lamont Poetry Selection for 1955, and was generously praised everywhere. It was a book of great charm and wit, its assurance and amusement always apparent. The present volume in comparison might be thought solemn. It is, rather, a superbly brave attempt not to repeat the triumph of the first book but to try for something even more difficult: a steady and appraising vision which is earned in art as in life only at great cost.' Were you consciously making it new in your second book, not wanting to be caught resting on your laurels?

I'm happy to be reminded of Hecht's review. Certainly I was trying to make it new in the second book. In particular, I reacted to the stringencies of Kunitz and Arrowsmith. *Exiles and Marriages* was ingratiating, and I wanted to stop that stuff. *The Dark Houses* is darker.

By 1956 I began to feel uncomfortable in the iambic. All I could think about was writing in iambics, making a witty metre. I had painted myself into a corner. My problems had nothing to do with the nature of traditional English verse but the nature of my associations with it. I started to try writing syllabics. The first I wrote was a poem called 'Je suis une table' – a language error – really about feeling as inarticulate as a table. Syllabics was a way of holding on to number while avoiding iambic. I rhymed on the off-stress, pretending that English was French. From syllabics I took the leap to various types of free verse. I felt this necessity to break out of the cage I had made for myself, even before *Howl.*

The day that Allen Ginsberg died, there was a tribute to Jane [Kenyon] in Washington, several of us on the platform. I was the last to speak. The younger people all told what a liberation it had been for them when *Howl* came out, showing them another way. When my turn came, I said, 'Well, when *Howl* came out I thought that it was the worst thing that had ever been written! I had tenure in iambic pentameter.' I had grown up with the New Critical orthodoxy that didn't know what to do with things like *Howl.* Or with Hardy. So I saved them for later.

How much of an influence on your new work was Bly?

I think that what I was doing was quite different from Bly's work. But he and I would meet and criticize each other's work, or do it by mail. We've done it for fifty years. It's a friendship of opposites. Bly always tells – if we're on a programme together – that he would send me a poem that disclosed the secrets of the universe and that I would write back to him and say: that period should be a semi-colon and you should not break the line there, you should break it here. And your grammar's wrong. He says I would send him a draft of a poem and he would write back: you ought to have a dragon in the second stanza. He's Jungian and I'm Freudian; he's Plato and I'm Aristotle; he's Don Quixote and I'm Sancho Panza. When we are together, we exaggerate these differences.

You had this forty-eight hour rule.

Bly is always deciding things. He decided we should reply to each other's poems within forty-eight hours. Sometimes I accuse him of changing it to the forty-eight day rule. We have tended to work together. It happened in our generation. Eventually Galway Kinnell and I worked together.

We have a hazy grasp of Kinnell. He was here for last year's Poetry International.

I like him.

Clive James wrote a review of something he did a few years ago – The Avenue Bearing the Initial of Christ into the New World *– calling it 'the long Ezra Pound poem that Pound himself could never have written.' Was Kinnell a part of* The Sixties *thing?*

He was to the side, not in the centre of it. But he also moved away from metre – from Yeats to Whitman.

I met him for the first time in Bly's apartment. Carol and Robert would take an apartment in New York while somebody went to Florida, about a month in New York. Kinnell and I got talking, poetry, literature. After a while Galway said to me, 'I used to hate you.' *Exiles and Marriages* pissed off a lot of people. Galway and I became close friends.

Bly was very keen on translation, but this seems never to have had very much interest for you. Not everyone's attracted by translation, of course, but it's quite common amongst poets who endure dry spells, and you've had one or two of those.

I translated some poems from the Spanish. With help. Maybe ten or fifteen. But, no, I never felt that I had another language securely enough. I did Horace, at Harvard, with a prose trot. I used the same prose trot when I did the unHoratian adaptations from the first book of the *Odes* in *The Museum of Clear Ideas*. When I find it difficult to get started on new poems, I have tended to engage in some ongoing parody or nonsense that I can fiddle with. Playing with words.

The Fifties *turned into* The Sixties, *and* The Sixties *turned into* The Seventies. *What happened then, because* The Seventies *never turned into* The Eighties, *did it?*

Editing a magazine becomes tiresome – as you know. I don't think that there was an issue of *The Eighties*.

What about Dickey? You knew him too, didn't you?

I knew Dickey. I brought Dickey to Wesleyan. It was dangerous to know Dickey.

Why was that? Dangerous with his crossbow and arrow?

Oh, he was someone who could never forgive a favour. Bly promoted him and Jim later put knives in his back. I was Jim's editor at Wesleyan. I quit the Wesleyan board just as I was finishing editing his third book. I had sent him the manuscript of my third collection, *A Roof of Tiger Lilies*, and he'd written me a letter praising it greatly and then, after I stopped being his editor, he reviewed it in *The American Scholar* and gave it hell. It pissed me off at the time but by now it seems funny. Later, when he had the poetry chair at the Library of Congress, he had me along to read with Bill Stafford. Jim got terribly drunk and we stood behind the curtains while we waited for them to open, and Jim said, 'Isn't this a grand thing to do for your country?' What on earth did he mean by that?

He's the only guy I've ever seen in real life take off his stetson and throw it so that it landed on the hook. I mean, how many times do you think he practised at that?

I spent a week with him once when he was at Reed College. At first I thought he was a friend. He asked me to be his literary executor, and later I found out that he had asked a number of other poets at the same time. He was a terrific liar. That visit, we were driving along and I said, 'What was the best thing you did in the War, Jim?' And he said, 'It was the time I shot down two unarmed Japanese transports. They just sat there in the air like ducks and I shot one down and curved away, gave the other a little time to think about it, and then I shot that one down too. Lots of men died that day.' I knew when I asked the question I would get a lie. Later I said to him, 'You know, Jim, I think the best quality in the world is loyalty, don't you?' And he said, 'No, I think it's the worst.' We knew what we were talking about. He praised Bly to the skies in print, and when I met him for the first time I said, 'I'm glad you like Bly so much. I like him too.' He said, 'Oh, he's no good.' Jim told me about the time during the War he married an Australian girl, and he was off fighting in the Pacific when she died. None of it was true. Still, I love some of his early stuff: 'The Heaven of Animals'. Remember that?

Yes, the gentle Dickey.

With the later grandomania of the stewardess poem and the 'May Day Sermon', it became typing.

When I met him he'd just had a big success with his novel, Deliverance, *so he was being Burt Reynolds, you know. He was in the movie, as the sheriff. He took me out to a lake and he had a crossbow with him. He said: 'Look at all this: it's so big, so goddam big. And no cocksucking English critic is going to tell me that it isn't.'*

He was funny. Bullying and posturing and so on.

Remember the interview he did for The Paris Review? *Damning almost everybody, including Frost: 'If it were thought that anything I wrote was influenced by Robert Frost, I would take that particular work of mine, shred it, and flush it down the toilet, hoping not to clog the pipes.'*

He attacked Frost elsewhere as well. If you read the *Letters* you will see him praising first and then attacking. He had some smart things to say about poetry but most of his letters are self-serving. He attacked Frost partly because Frost was a northerner, but mostly because Frost was on the top of the American heap.

When I visited him, he had a table with all his own works spread out individually. We went from room to room and looked at his works, and then we went into a study area where he played blue grass music very loud. After that we went out to the lakeside where he had this crossbow and intoned lessons on manhood and how to be a great American poet, and so on. It was quite extraordinary.

I once told him I never had wanted to play football because I was afraid of pain. And he said, with disdain, 'I've never understood that.'

I mentioned A Roof of Tiger Lilies *and* The Alligator Bride *just now. A number of critics complained about their surrealist experimentalism, one saying that '[t]he language sounds constricted and self-conscious, the insights no deeper than those generated only by casual observation,' another, rather later, calling it 'a sort of versified Method Acting mumble.' Both sought to excuse what you were doing on the grounds that you were searching for a way out of an impasse. How do you feel about those volumes now? Do you have any sympathy for what these critics were saying?*

Well, I was trying to get away from iambic; I was trying to reach something like a language of dream. But I don't really understand what they mean. They have a right to dislike the poems. But I like some of them at least. Maybe there are too many slight, small surprises. I like 'The Alligator Bride', and 'The Long River' (maybe Jane's favourite poem of mine, written when she was only ten years old) and 'The Man in the Dead Machine'. But what do I know?

You're much less involved in the literary-political stuff than you used to be. In the early 1960s you were very active in all that. Did you just get fed up with it?

In those days, I took sides. I admired certain poets and promoted them and put them in anthologies. Is that *politics*? It was advocacy. It wasn't favour-trading. With *The Paris Review,* and the anthologies, I was trying to establish a taste for what I loved. I continued to edit the Michigan Series. I worked for *Harvard* magazine and so on until cancer started hitting me. I quit everything after my second cancer, which I wasn't supposed to survive. That was six and a half years ago. (I'm now cured.) And these days I'd rather stay alone and write, and write letters to people than meet them. I have an enormous correspondence.

You've talked of the 1960s as a really low stretch in your life. That was really to do with the ill health? You wrote much less then.

Middle and late '60s. It wasn't ill health, not physical ill health. I wrote less and drank more. My separation from my first wife happened in '67, and my divorce in '69. I married Jane in '72. I was writing less and I was aware I was not writing so well as earlier, though a writer is never a good judge of his own work. In '64 or '66 I wrote 'The Man in the Dead Machine', and for the next seven or eight years I never wrote anything that I thought was up to it. Maybe 'The Alligator Bride', or perhaps that was earlier.

How bad was the drinking problem? I mean compared to, say, Berryman's? In the 1960s it was almost required for poets to be, well, self-destructive.

I was miserable and I compounded the misery with drink, a pretty common phenomenon. There was a time when I never went to bed without drinking at least a bottle of whisky and taking two Nembutals. If I did that now I'd be dead.

You were on your own at that point?

Yes. For five years. I'd go to parties and drink soda water, then go home and drink a bottle of scotch because if I drank at parties I'd fall over, and probably drag someone with me. But no, it wasn't as bad as Berryman or Thomas or Dickey or Wright.

Did it affect your job? Because you were still teaching at Ann Arbor then, weren't you?

I never had a drink before a class. I only remember getting drunk once before a reading, and being unable to read the page. I came out of it gradually with Jane's help. Jane wasn't into prohibition; she drank along with me, but less. I met her in '69.

She was a student?

Yes. I wasn't attracted to her at first. I liked her: she was smart, funny, and I was fond of her – as other people in the class were. A year or so later she was living with a guy who wanted to marry her. She was sceptical. Then she left him and I heard from a mutual friend that, although it was she who broke up, she was wretched. I called her up and asked her out. The first few dates all she could talk about was this guy. I had many girlfriends at the time, terrified of getting married again. But my girlfriends gradually dropped away. When Jane and I first talked about marriage, after about ten months of dating, we dismissed it because she was so much younger. She would be a widow for twenty-five years. After we married, we lived in Ann Arbor three years. It was okay – academic parties, dinners – but she wanted to give it up and move to New Hampshire. I resigned my tenure in 1975 to take the freelance life. Her parents were freelancers. Talking about my giving up tenure later, she said, 'It was easy for *me* to say!'

Her parents were writers, were they?

No, musicians. Her father jammed with Bix Beiderbecke in 1930.

So at what point did the poetry start to flow again?

It was in 1972 that I had the onslaught of lines that twelve or fourteen years later turned into part of *The One Day*. In 1974, after two years being married to Jane, when the drinking had decreased, I started writing 'Kicking the Leaves', making a sound different from anything I had done before.

So it was before you moved back to New Hampshire?

Just before. In 'Kicking the Leaves', it seems as if I knew I was going to move away. But it wasn't a conscious prophecy.

So the New Hampshire farm – you went with Jane to show her. Who lived there then?

My grandmother.

And your grandfather?

My grandfather died when I was at Oxford. 1953. My grandmother lived on until '75, when she was ninety-seven.

When did your father die?

1955.

So your father and grandfather died within two years of each other?

57

Yes, my father wrote me at Oxford about my grandfather's death and he died two and half years later. My mother lived to be almost ninety-one.

The women lived on.

Jane didn't. My mother made it only to ninety years and eleven months because she smoked two packs of Kents a day.

If she'd made it three, she'd perhaps be here today. I notice you smoke Kents.

I actually converted her to Kents. The end of the first marriage was very bad. I had two children and I thought I would never divorce. But I felt like the skeleton in the cockpit. From the age of thirty-five to thirty-seven I couldn't write poems. The first year I thought I was taking a holiday; the second year I knew I would never write again. Depression and drinking. The best thing I ever did, aside from marrying Jane, was leaving the academic world and heading north.

It was Jane's suggestion that you gave up academia?

Yes. I took her to the farmhouse in Wilmot after we were married and she adored it. When we came back to Ann Arbor, we drove about looking at farmhouses for sale and she said: 'It's stupid to buy a farm here when there's New Hampshire.' Of course her suggestion sounded silly – because it would be a long commute from New Hampshire to teach in Ann Arbor. We were thinking of spending the summers there, perhaps early retirement. We had no idea at that point of giving up tenure and moving here permanently. In 1975 I had made enough money from a textbook to take a year's leave without pay, and we decided to camp out in the farm for one year. My grandmother had gone into the old folks' home because she was incontinent, and turned up the kerosene, burning things. In order to pay for her care my mother would mortgage the house; instead I mortgaged it, and, as I say, we camped out there for a year. When we arrived at the old place, my grandmother took a turn for the worse, as if she knew that the house would be taken care of. I held her hand while she died. It was August. By October Jane said, 'I'm not going back. I'll chain myself to the root cellar.' I resigned my Professorship and the university department wouldn't accept it, giving me another year's leave. But I knew what I was going to do. The first year I felt fairly frantic; I had no idea where the money was going to come from – for mortgage, for tuition fees for my children. I worked very hard, and loved it, and made a living. I have been accused of self-discipline. It's not true, because I loved what I was doing. I worked on poems first thing in the

58

morning, which is when I feel clearest. I'd write poems first because that was when I was more likely to cross things out. Later I would turn to prose: a children's book, an article for a magazine, a textbook.

The poems changed again, didn't they?

Yes, they began to change before I moved. It began in '72, while I was still at Ann Arbor, with the manic onslaught of lines that became, years later, books one and two of *The One Day*. Certainly things changed with 'Kicking the Leaves', in 1974.

Kicking the Leaves *contains some of the poems for which you're perhaps best known: the title poem, 'Maple Syrup', 'Ox Cart Man', 'Names of Horses'. You've been asked about these many times over, and have probably said as much as you want to, so let me ask about another of the book's pieces, 'Flies'. It's a longish prose poem, in eight sections, and very affecting. Like the poems I just mentioned, it confronts head-on the hard truth that 'one generation passeth away, and another generation cometh', prompted in this instance by the death of your grandmother. It's very effective, but can I ask why you opted for prose here? To the best of my knowledge, you'd only done this once before, in a very different kind of poem, 'The Presidentiad'.*

I'm glad you take an interest in 'Flies'. I like that poem and nobody ever talks about it. I will tell you why I opted for prose. I wrote 'Flies' in lines, and worked it over a long time. When I showed it to friends I had a response from two of them on the same day – I think it was James Wright and Louis Simpson, but I might be wrong – and both suggested that I turn it into prose. I liked it – though I don't generally enjoy the prose poem; I am too much in love with lines and line breaks. Sometimes I think about turning 'Flies' back into lines.

After Kicking the Leaves *came* The Happy Man, *which was published by Random House. It was the only one of your collections to be published by them. Since this broke a pattern – your first three collections had been published by Viking, your second three by Harper & Row – can I ask what happened? The book was well reviewed, wasn't it? It also won the Lenore Marshall Prize.*

Publishing is crazy in the United States. I was with Harper and Row for sixteen or seventeen years, and had a marvellous editor, Fran McCullough. Her authors won a Pulitzer, a National Book Award. She was Plath's editor. There was a change of bosses and they summoned her into an office and fired her in fifteen minutes. So I swore I would never publish another book with them. I was going to follow her to another house, when I had a book ready, but by the time I had a book ready the other house had been discontinued by its parent company. I looked around. There was a young editor I liked at Random House, Jonathan Galassi, and I took the book to him. Then Random House more or less committed suicide. A month before the book was due to come out, Jon wrote me that he was resigning. He gave me to another editor, rather fashionable at the time, who wrote me immediately telling me that he was also resigning. I was given to a third editor, of whom I had never heard, and I telephoned her. 'This thing was dumped on my desk last Friday,' she sweetly told me. I offered to fly down to New York and meet her and she told me not to come. It was published with no support – but then, as you say, it did fairly well.

The last poem in The Happy Man *is 'The Day I Was Older', whose title derives from an event recalled in the fourth of its five stanzas:*

> *Last night at suppertime I outlived my father, enduring*
> *the year, month, day, and hour*
> *when he lay back on a hospital bed in the guestroom*
> *among cylinders of oxygen – mouth open, nostrils and lips*
> *fixed unquivering, pale blue. Now I have wakened*
> *more mornings to frost whitening the grass,*
> *read the newspaper more times, and stood more times,*
> *my hand on the doorknob without opening the door.*
> *Father of my name, father of long fingers, I remember*
> *your dark hair, and your face almost unwrinkled.*

Did it really happen like that, with you waiting for the moment?

No, I lied. I was with my grandmother Kate when she died, holding her hand; I was with Jane; but I was not with my father. I was living in Cambridge then, visiting him once a week, and due to come down the next morning. When my uncle telephoned to say that my father would die soon, I suggested that I drive down right then – but he said that I should wait until the morning. He died at about six at night. It was not difficult to imagine the scene.

The One Day *you were working on for a long time?*

I put those lines in a drawer for years. They frightened me. At first, when I came back to New Hampshire, I felt at one with the neighbours and the landscape. I knew I was not a New Hampshirite – I was from the suburbs – but I had chosen this place. I knew what I was doing. I felt joy in being part of this landscape and culture. I think I was writing for the neighbours, to the neighbours, and the writing was far more accessible, the poetry. Eventually I realized that writing for the neighbours was another limitation, but in the meantime I had had a clear run at it. Afterwards, I could write *The One Day*. I took the old lines out of the drawer and set to work. I needed again to change, to keep moving.

But before that, you'd been writing more prose?

I wrote prose to make a living. I'd written prose earlier, as you know, but now I was writing for magazines, textbooks, eventually children's books. These books paid the mortgage. I tried to build an estate for Jane's widowhood. Always poetry made up twenty, twenty-five percent of my income, mostly the poetry readings.

One of the prose things you produced before the move to New Hampshire was Henry Moore: The Life and Work of a Great Sculptor. *Moore was someone you came to hold in very high esteem, wasn't he? As much for his ambition as his accomplishment?*

I came to admire his achievement very much. When I was an undergraduate at Harvard, I pinned to my wall a Penguin print of a Moore drawing. Then I first saw the large sculpture when I came to the Festival of Britain in 1951. An American magazine asked me to interview him in 1959, when I was first living in Thaxted and looking for freelance work. Talking with him was wonderful. He and Irina came to our Thaxted house for dinner. I spent one solid day with him, and many times I saw him for two or three hours. I loved the way he talked about sculpture. Every time he said something, I immediately transferred what he was saying to poetry. I think he was quoting Rodin when he said, 'Never think of a surface except as the extension of a volume.' I took it off and ran with it. I learned more about poetry from Henry Moore than I did from the old poets. I did indeed love his attitude toward work, and toward the life of work, and toward the seriousness of his ambition – to compete, not with Barbara Hepworth, but with Michelangelo.

That year in Thaxted, 1959-60, I wrote my first prose book, *String Too Short To Be Saved*. Part came out in the *New Yorker*. Before I left England, I told Moore I would like to write more about him, and he was agreeable. When Mr Shawn, the *New Yorker*'s editor, asked if I would like to write more prose for them (they'd done my poems since 1954) I said, 'How about a profile of Henry Moore?' He checked to see if anybody had dibs on him, then told me to go ahead. It was difficult. *String* was memoir, this was objective prose. From Thaxted in 1963-64 I drove to interview sculptors and dealers and museum people and Moore's old

61

friends. I didn't begin to get it right until the fourth draft. The third was *hopeless*. Shawn rejected it, but gave me the advice that turned me around. They published it in two long parts, and Harper and Row (and Gollancz) made it a book the next year.

Did Moore read the book?

Moore read it. He read it in manuscript and denied vehemently having said one sentence to a friend of his. I took it out.

You spoke a moment ago about all the readings you used to give. They must have obliged you to roam the country a bit?

I'd be gone maybe forty nights a year. Still am.

What kind of fees? The average, say. What fee wouldn't you accept?

I read for nothing sometimes. If someone writes and says, 'Would you read for us? What do you charge?' now I say $3,000. Earlier, it was $1,000, $2,000. If they say, '$3,000 is too much. We've got $2,000,' then I frequently do it.

And expenses?

Yes: airfare, motel, and so on. One time a small college in Arkansas got me through an agency that called me up and asked what I charged and I said, 'What do *you* get? Get me as much as you can.' I netted $5,600. (Maya Angelou gets $35,000, I understand.) When I went to this little college, they gave me a great poetry-reading story. I was picked up in Tulsa, Oklahoma, to be driven to Arkansas by the Dean of Humanities, a sweet man who loved poetry, and a Dean of Honours, who had contracted for me – feisty and warm. I flew in at night because in the morning I would read at a compulsory gathering of students. We stopped for supper on the way. I went to the men's room and when I came back I heard the Dean of Honours saying [attempts accent] 'Well, I'm going to tell him.' She turned and said, sweetly, 'Donald, if you say "fuck" in chapel tomorrow I'm fired.' I said, 'You won't have to worry about a thing. But can I tell this story?' She said, 'You go right ahead, Donald.' I read in New Hampshire, at the meeting house in Canaan, at schools, in town libraries – usually for nothing. At a Canaan reading, the guy who ran it brought his two daughters. I read my 'Letter at Christmas' from *Without* which ends up talking about how Jane used to look out the window and I would press into her. This first Christmas after her death, I say, I press my penis against the sink. A day after the reading, the little girls were having supper with their parents and the seven-year-old asked, 'Why did Donald Hall press himself into the sink like that? Didn't it hurt?' Her father said, 'Well you know how you like to touch yourself there? Men do too.' She said, 'Oh.' Later, she lifted up her frankfurter and said, 'Like Donald Hall, I press my weiner into the mustard.'

Do you do readings on your own? I know you did them with Jane some-times.

Jane and I did many, the last years of her life. Mostly I read alone, occasionally with other poets. With three hundred or so days of silence and solitude, I like a few days of human contact.

But do you enjoy doing readings?

Yes. Before I decided to become a poet at fourteen, I thought of the stage. The actor side comes out in readings. I don't perform the poems like an actor but I do use the voice.

Are American poets expected to be good at projecting their poems?

I don't know. Some read well and others not.

In England quite a few poets mumble their poems. It's almost like a sign of integrity that you don't perform, hold forth.

Bloody English fear of seeming to be eager or excited! I don't think anyone ever missed a syllable of mine.

Can we go back to The One Day? *You say somewhere that your grasp of what you were doing while working on that was enhanced by an observation of David Shapiro's, made in a review of* The Happy Man, *which contained what was to become the poem's first section, 'Shrubs Burned Away'. He described your work as 'a kind of psalm to the passage, as Freud put it, from hysterical misery to ordinary unhappiness.' What did you take him to mean by that? And how exactly did it help? I mean, did it enable to you to see how existing material should be assembled, or did it actually give rise to new material?*

David has never been able to find me the source of that quote – but it does sound like Freud. I liked the distinction. The best possible condition is 'ordinary unhappiness' and that gave me the happy ending to *The One Day*. There's an inherent problem with living: no matter how extreme happiness may be, it is never so intense as pain and loss.

*Am I right in thinking that your mother got to see 'Shrubs Burned Away',
and that she thought you were writing about her in there?*

There are a man and a woman in that poem, and the woman's mother
was alcoholic. My mother kept asking me if I thought she had been
alcoholic. I didn't. For a brief patch, my mother and father tried drinking
too much, but it didn't last very long. Maybe she was thinking of that
time.

The One Day *received a great deal of praise. Hayden Carruth called it
your 'very best work ... complex, solid and very habitable ... [a] considerable work of art', and Thom Gunn said, 'this poem ... may indeed be
seen as the synthesis of a whole life's work. It is one of those books, like
Elizabeth Bishop's last collection, which alters the way we look at the
jumbled contents of the poetic career preceding it, giving it retrospectively a shape, a pattern, a consistency it didn't seem to have at the
time.' It also won from the National Book Critics Circle Award, of course.
What are your feelings about the poem, this many years on?*

Maybe *The One Day* is the best thing I have done. I would prefer that
Without were, for obvious reasons. I worked on *The One Day* for a long,
long time, and was pleased with it. Still am. At this point, I find the third
section a bit complacent – 'ordinary unhappiness' is too happy – but I
still like the first two parts. Back when I had an attack of bipolarity, a
year after Jane died, as I was coming up from the bottom I wrote an
angry poem – in the old ten line stanza – that took back the happy
ending of the third book of *The One Day*. It's called 'Kill the Day'. A
magazine called *Gettysburg* will publish it soon.

I quoted Thom Gunn just now, talking about what, prior to The One
Day, *had looked to him like 'the jumbled contents' of your poetic career. Would you have had any sympathy with such a description, back
then? Or has it always seemed to you that your poetic career has been of
a piece?*

Thom finds that my work went up and down, back and forth – and why
not? I guess I would perfectly well agree with 'the jumbled contents' –
though Thom and I might disagree on which poems were better and
which worse. I don't think my poetic life has been of a piece. I'm not
sure anyone's is.

Not everyone liked The One Day. *Fred Chappell, reviewing* Old and
New Poems, *called it 'an admirable attempt [at a contemporary epic],
but hobbled by muddy organization and some puffy rhetoric.' Chappell*

is by no means an ill-disposed critic. His chief criticism, if I can put it at its most general, seems to be that you are apt on occasion to write beyond your means, but this is a vice he's not inclined to be too hard on because he thinks it has its roots in something admirable: 'He seems willing to try almost anything. He must foresee that a great deal of what he attempts will fail, yet he goes right ahead and gives it his best shot.'

Was Fred actually talking about *The One Day* in that review, or just the *Old and New Poems*? Of course I don't mean *The One Day* to have either 'muddy organization' or 'puffy rhetoric', but perhaps it does. Chappell is a candid friend.

How do you meet other poets in the States?

There are festivals; we may read separately but we meet. If you teach at a college and organize the readings, you meet the people you invite – which can sometimes be favour-trading of course.

Do you think this professionalism has had an effect on poetry? You know, if you give someone a harsh review you might be damaging his livelihood? The more professional the poetry business gets, the softer the reviewing, it seems.

Reviewing in America now is just terrible. Who is the reviewer of any standing in the United States today? Helen Vendler? She has no taste. Sometimes she admires people who are good, but there are others. She's not adventurous.

Is she powerful?

She has prizes and fellowships in her pocket. She appears to cherish power. If she were a better judge ... She's a competent writer of prose, but ... It's strange: the popularity of poetry has increased as reviewing or criticism has diminished. Forty years ago, the fifteen best known poets in the United States were printed in editions of one thousand, hardback, which they might sell out in three years if they were lucky. But they might be reviewed by Louise Bogan, Malcolm Cowley, Conrad Aiken, Edmund Wilson. Now who are the reviewers? *The New York Times* has always been bad. The *New York Review of Books* seldom does books of verse. I was fortunate enough to have John Bayley do *Without*. Anyway, the same poets, as it were – now it might be the best twenty-five – sell 10,000 copies rather than one. Without much public attention by reviewers. By and large, the reviews are written by people who believe in 'Boost, don't knock.' They all have something nice to say. Very little negative criticism. I reviewed Robert Penn Warren in the *New York Review of Books* – no, *New York Times* – and gave him hell. Letters flooded in: 'Why did you do this?' I also blasted late Lowell.

More than once.

Yes, I wrote about him for you.

Yes, you said that Notebook *was written with one eye on Stockholm, or words to that effect.*

I still love early Lowell, *Lord Weary* and two poems in *Mills of the Kavanaghs*: 'Mother Theresa,' 'Falling Asleep over the Aeneid'. Parts of *Life Studies* and the title poem of *For the Union Dead*.

He wrote too much.

Nine books in the last ten years.

How would you explain this move to 'positive' as opposed to 'negative' reviewing in the United States. Here too, I'd say.

I've heard it said it's just a form of favour-trading. But I've seen little evidence. Maybe fear? I've seen favours traded in other ways. There's one guy who edits a series of poets for an academic press who's published three major editors of our time, all three of whom have published scandalously bad poems by this editor in their magazines. I'm sure they tell themselves they really *like* each other. There is a notoriously nasty reviewer named William Logan, but he's so nasty he's comic.

I suppose if everybody else knows what they are doing, it's not so bad.

James Dickey once said to Robert Penn Warren, 'Let's keep on giving each other prizes.'

It's the only way.

Maybe. At least he said it openly.

There's an interesting remark of Ransom's, from fairly late on in his career: 'Criticism is quite presumptuous, and I give it more and more reluctantly; I don't think it's quite a good man's business to do too much of it because it results in one of two ways: he commits gross injustices, or he is drawn too much out of his bias and nature by the effort of understanding and sympathy.' Do you have any sympathy with that?

Yes, I suppose I do. I have never been a good poetry reviewer. Maybe I did best writing out of Thaxted for the *New Statesman*, almost forty years ago. *Lupercal*, a late Auden; I can't remember. I liked it because for a year or so I had a regular soapbox, and I felt I could develop ideas. Perhaps I have gone too much in both directions that Ransom mentions – in outrage and in sympathy. I've wanted to attack bad work by good poets, like late Lowell, or bad work by celebrated bad poets, like Robert Penn Warren.

There's an assumption among the young poets in Britain that all poets are equal because there's no real way of judging.

There's an assumption in the USA that all poetry began in 1974. Or, pick your year. When a young poet visited me, I started to quote Wyatt, 'They flee from me...' She'd never heard of the poem. That ignorance is frustrating. I'm not talking about stupid people.

But is poetry very local, regionalized in the States? You've got your State laureates, your leading poets of the eastern seaboard, poets of the North-west. Where's the centre reckoned to be?

There is no centre. People call me a New Hampshire poet. Every adjective is a diminishment: women poets; men poets; black poets.

New Hampshire pastoralists?

People literally say that I remind them of Robert Frost! I deplore regionalism, but it is an international phenomenon now, nations breaking apart at the seams. Emphasis on American regions is a way of dealing with the multiplicity of poems. There are so many 'poets'. If you break them up, subdivide them, it's possible to read almost all of a category. That's an excuse for it. But I hate it. Let there be one American poetry, and let the best poets stand out.

What would the optimum USA poetic career now be? Getting prize X, a Pulitzer, appearing in The New Yorker, *getting reviewed by Helen Vendler?*

Are you using the word 'career'?

Yes.

Winning a MacArthur, a National Book Award, a Pulitzer, being unavoidable to anthologists – and being the subtitle of a Vendler collection. Jorie Graham had two subtitles in a row, then got the Boylston Chair at Harvard after Seamus Heaney, an appointment doubtless in Vendler's power. Graham is good, but she doesn't stand out that much.

So the power is less to do with her reviewing and more to do with her patronage?

I don't think she judges for the Guggenheim every year, but she has done. The Pulitzer is hers.

There was a time, though, when the kind of power you say Vendler has amassed would almost inevitably have created some vigorous opposition to challenge it.

I don't think there is nowadays. I've been known to insult her, I'm happy to say. Tony Hecht did it brilliantly. But, I've known people who dislike her and her criticism but have refrained from confrontation – have even written her letters of praise. Corrupt. 'Oh, well, I'm a hypocrite about that,' they say.

You've been very scathing about poetry workshops, at least as these are typically organized in the States: 'Although in theory workshops serve a useful purpose in gathering young artists together, workshop practices enforce the McPoem', this being your name for the verse equivalent of a well-known variety of hamburger, 'identical from coast to coast and in all the little towns in between, subject to the quality control of the least common denominator.' If I understand you, it's the separation of creative writing and literature that's at the root of the problem, so that workshops of the kind famously run by Winters in Stanford – which you yourself attended, of course – or by Engle in Iowa, constitute significant exceptions?

Winters's workshop was not the workshop as we know it. It was serious, ambitious, and dominated by Winters. We four met in his office. You handed him a poem and he would read it aloud and then immediately deliver a little essay on it. There would be discussion but little argument.

I don't know how the separation of creative writing and literature happened. When I went to Michigan, I taught literature almost entirely. I went there on the condition that I not teach creative writing. After teaching freshman composition a couple of times, I asked to teach creative writing. I loved teaching literature, because I learned so much. I deplore the separation. For the English major, I think it is good if teachers come from different places: some who concentrate on historical backgrounds or biographical; some, like a poet, who concentrates on how poems are made, on sounds and metaphors. Oh, there has been snobbery on both sides. The later domination of English departments by theorists accounts for some of the more recent separation. Sometimes now the only places within the university which teach literature as literature are the creative writing departments. It's a shame.

As I understand it, the separation of creative writing and literature came about as the result of antagonisms between the faculty in formerly unified departments. Donald Justice, who taught at the Iowa workshop for many years, told Dana Gioia: 'I remember that innocent time when all we wanted was to be separate from the academic side, separate but equal. We were not equal; we were condescended to; we had reason to feel beleaguered.' Where did all that antagonism come from, do you think?

I didn't experience what Don Justice talks about. I found envy, from professors who published little. And I took time away from teaching – fellowships, saving money from readings – which annoyed some of them.

Mightn't a part of the problem with the poetry workshops be that there are too many of them? Not so long ago, someone worked out that there were 200 of the things, set to produce 20,000 graduates within the decade? If it's true that you need to be a decent poet if you're to teach others how to write decent poetry, there surely aren't enough to go around?

One friend called the epidemic of workshops a Ponzi scheme. You teach poets to teach poets to teach poets. There are thousands of people out there who are supposed to be qualified to teach writing. There are just not that many jobs. Mind you, workshops bring young aspirants together, which can help. And trying to write, even if you fail, teaches you to read with more intelligence.

You've said that the best critics of poetry are almost all poets. The one exception I seem to remember your allowing is Hazlitt. No other exceptions?

I cannot think of another exception. Yes, Harold Bloom. Not all the time.

Tell me about your illness? It was 1990, wasn't it, that ...

1989. I had the top of my colon out. Cancer. There's a blood test called the CEA that was checked at regular intervals for recurrence. Three is a passing grade. It was 1.4; 2.4; 2.6; 2.8; 2.1; 1.2. Then in 1992 the number was 37! I had a CAT scan, ultrasound. I looked at the screen myself and in the right hemisphere of the liver was something that big. [Rounds out index fingers and thumbs.] The ultrasound technician said, 'Oh, it looks like an hourglass.' It was colon cancer of the liver. The other hemisphere appeared to be clear. Many times cancer metastasises to both sides of the liver, and there's not much you can do. In my case, they couldn't find any sign of cancer in the left lobe, so they operated to remove the right two thirds of the liver. The artery too. The remaining side expands to fill the space and increase cell numbers. The liver continues to function. My liver function tests now are as normal as if I had a whole liver. It was assumed that I would die, that the other side would develop cancer. I had chemotherapy after the second operation, not the first. Perhaps that helped. At any rate, the cancer did not return. The operation was six and a half years ago, and after five years you're considered okay. Jane and I spent a long time planning for her widowhood.

There were poems by her about this?

Yes. 'Otherwise' is thinking of my death. And 'Afternoon at MacDowell'. 'Pharaoh' may be the best. These are the last two stanzas:

> Home again, we live as charily as strangers.
> Things are off: Touch rankles, food
> is not good. Even the kindness of friends
> turns burdensome; their flowers sadden
> us, so many and so fair.
>
> I woke in the night to see your
> diminished bulk lying beside me –
> you on your back, like a sarcophagus
> as your feet held up covers ...
> The things you might need in the next
> life surrounded you – your comb and glasses,
> water, a book and a pen.

How long between your feeling that you were going to live and knowing that she might not?

I did not pass the five-year mark until a year after her death. I was terrified, when we knew that she was ill, that my cancer would come back and I wouldn't be able to help her.

So you hadn't actually thought of yourself then as recovering?

In '93 I felt fine but I was waiting for the cancer to return. In January of '94 Jane's leukaemia arrived. She lived until April of 1995. It was only during the last eleven days that we *knew* she was going to die. She had a bone marrow transplant; it worked in itself – the new marrow engrafted – but six months after the transplant the leukaemia came back and nothing more could be done.

So you had eleven days in which you knew. And five of those days were spent arranging her poems?

Not quite five. The fifth day she was beginning to lose words, anoxia I presume. She could begin a sentence but not finish it. We did virtually all the work on *Otherwise* during days two and three. We also wrote her obituary together and planned the church service. I tried to think of everything, but I never talked to her about the monument. Later, I knew what I wanted. I wanted polished black granite with white lettering. I didn't know why I wanted that, but about two months after it was in place I suddenly remembered the Vietnam War Memorial in Washington that Jane and I both admired. On the stone I quote two lines from Jane's MacDowell poem: 'I believe in the miracles of art but what / prodigy will keep you safe beside me ...' My name is carved beside hers, and the date of my birth. That's when I'll be safe beside her!

There were other deaths too ...

My mother died two months into Jane's disease, but she was old and ready to die. Then Jane's mother Polly died. For the first four months of Jane's illness, Polly was just fine, a great help. She lived nearby, and when Jane needed the help of two people she would move in. As soon as Jane could cope, with me alone, her mother would leave. She had respect for our privacy. Marvellous woman. Then in the summer Polly developed cancer of the lung that got into the rib-bones. Nothing to do except radiation. Jane was all set to go to Seattle that October for the BMT, and her mother was going to come with us for radiation. Two dying women! In September of 1993, just before we were to fly away, Jane's leukaemia returned, a relapse. New Hampshire had to get her into a second remission before she could travel to Seattle, the mecca of the BMT. Meantime Polly needed to start radiation, so we left her behind. A house-sitter and good neighbours took care of her. Jane was in a wheelchair in Seattle when her mother died in January. We came back in February and Jane died in April. I forewarned many friends, the last eleven days. Jane's funeral was a great event, perhaps three hundred

71

people – many neighbours and cousins, many poets.

So you had ten, fifteen years of this writing life together?

Twenty years after we moved to New Hampshire.

I meant before your illness intervened and Jane's.

I was writing again two weeks after my operation.

So that was 1989.

Yes. '91 and '93 were good years. Especially '93.

How come?

Well, '92 was difficult because I had the operation and the chemotherapy. The best year of our lives was probably the year we remembered the least. But in 1993 we went to India, and performed a play for two actors called 'Love-Letters'. We did our only book-tour together. We read together a lot. Bill Moyers came and did a television documentary, mostly in January, which was shown in December.

Bill Moyers is a big celebrity in America, I gather. He is not very well known in Britain.

Bill Moyers was press secretary to Lyndon Johnson, now a film-maker for Public television. He's a man of enormous curiosity. He's done many programmes on poets, but poetry is only one of his interests. He decided to do Jane and me together, and began photographing us at a festival in 1992. Then he and his crew came to New Hampshire in January of '93. He spent two hours interviewing each of us. That night we did a reading in the town hall, so the film is full of reaction shots from neighbours. The television crew came to our church. They took thirty-five hours of tape to make a fifty-six minute film. When it was broadcast, December 1993, many people discovered Jane for the first time.

In January of 1994 the two of us read and lectured at Bennington in an MFA programme. We came home, and she began to feel bone pain, as if she were coming down with flu. After a nosebleed, she went to a local hospital which diagnosed the leukaemia. At Dartmouth-Hitchcock, a teaching hospital, they put her in remission quickly but they knew it wouldn't last. She had – there are four basic kinds of leukaemia; and I can't find out which sort Rilke had – Acute Lymphoblastic Leukaemia. ALL, the kind children usually get. Children often recover but when

72

adults get it it's not so likely. Her cancer also had what is called the Philadelphia Chromosome, which meant that no amount of chemo or radiation would check her leukaemia. It would always come back. The only way of staying alive was a bone-marrow transplant. It works sometimes, maybe twenty percent of the time, as I remember.

How was the donor found for Jane?

Her brother's antigens did not match. There's a national bank where many people's antigens are listed. The donor was a woman in Nebraska, the wife of a preacher in a small town. She had had troubles with general anaesthesia, which is needed, and donated her marrow anyway. We had no idea who she was at the time, nor she who Jane was. Three or four months after Jane died I wrote to the hospital. I said that I knew that the donor is not supposed to know if the donee dies. I wanted to give her Jane's books. One Sunday night I got a telephone call from Aurora, Nebraska – Ronda McCormick. I sent her Jane's books and she sent me pictures of her children. In 1997 I read poems in Nebraska and drove three hours to her house for lunch. After two hours, as we were leaving, her husband, Barry, said to me, 'It's good to get to meet, but there's one thing we want to know: do you always wear your shoes on the wrong feet?' These shoes are roomy because Jane got them when she was sick, a size too big. It was the only time I ever put them on the wrong feet. I told them, 'All poets do.' I'm sure that story's run all around their town.

You mentioned John Bayley's positive review of Without *earlier, which appeared in the* New York Review of Books. *Did you know that his own wife, Iris Murdoch, was seriously ill with Alzheimer's when he wrote that?*

No. I noticed that he listed Alzheimer's among diseases.

I was struck by a touching coincidence. Early on in Without, *there are some lines in which you talk about your working life at Eagle Pond Farm:*

> ...
> *Each morning we worked together*
> *apart, I in my downstairs study*
>
> *and Jane at her rolltop desk*
> *above the kitchen, making poems*
> ...

And in the first book Bayley wrote about his wife, Iris: A Memoir, *he describes their life together as one in which, until she fell ill, they drew 'closer and closer apart'.*

Jane's mind was good until the last four days, so we were not 'closer apart', until the very, very end. The months of her illness were the closest time of our lives. We had been very close anyway.

How has the book been received, generally?

As well as John Bayley's good review in the *New York Review of Books*, there were positive notices in *Poetry*, the *Boston Globe*, the *San Francisco Examiner, Atlantic* ... Some people had a hard time dealing with it, and I'm sure some people are offended by it.

Offended? By its nakedness?

Yes. Especially in the description of Jane's pain and her decline into death. I expected it. Recently I heard about one man who was enraged by it, not a reviewer. He called it 'exploitative'. I expected that reaction. I didn't think I was exploiting her in any way, and Jane wouldn't have thought so. She wrote 'Pharaoh'. Other people quite like the book but don't know what to say about it. I think it's hard to review. It has sold about 16,000 copies in hard cover – not going like *Birthday Letters*.

The title poem is very strange, isn't it? It's all the things I would expect myself to hate, not having any punctuation, and so on. But it's somehow very effective. How did the poem come about? It's very unlike you.

I can remember certain things about it coming to me. Once while Jane was in the hospital, I looked out the window and saw that the leaves were falling. I didn't even know they had come to the trees. A year without seasons. Then my mind made an analogy: a year without punctuation. I picked up a piece of paper and worked on it day after day. There is a moment in the writing of a poem when I suddenly think, 'I'm going to have it – it may take thirty to forty more drafts but I'm going to have this one.' With 'Without', I knew I would have it when I saw that the poem required a false dawn, or a conditional false dawn, in the next-to-last stanza. I wrote by her side; she was glad that somebody was writing. I wrote on other subjects also: narrative poems, third-person poems. I would speak them out, to record them for my assistant to make a clean copy, and Jane would hear bits and pieces. Sometimes she'd say, 'Read it out loud, Perkins.' I said, 'I've got this one that's about the leu-

74

kaemia.' We were never euphemistic. If anything, we had a tendency to look too directly at things, and call them by their names. I knew it was all right to read her 'Without'. Someone looking casually at that poem might think it was surrealism, but Janie said, 'That's how it is, Perkins.' The lack of punctuation and syntax expresses that year.

In an earlier interview, Anthony Hecht said that he couldn't write whilst in the middle of emotional turmoil. He could be hurt into poetry, but not before he'd had an opportunity to absorb the hurt, and to regain his balance. As Without *shows, that hasn't been your experience. I read you saying somewhere that working on* Without *was helping you to come to terms with what had happened, that you were* solving *your grief by putting it into sentences.*

I didn't solve my grief. The first drafts were all screaming. I needed to scream, out loud from time to time, and also on the page. Working on these pages helped me, revising, trying to turn the scream into the art of poetry. The grief did not go away, but for two hours a day I was happy, writing these poems of misery.

Going back to what you just said about the absence of punctuation, I thought much later of Paul Celan's 'Todesfuge', thought maybe that's where I remembered the device.

Really? I don't know it. What yours reminded me of was that prose thing of Tim O'Brien's, 'The Things they Carry'. It's incantatory in this style but it doesn't have the no-punctuation device. Anyway, the poem's very moving. – Why 'Perkins', incidentally?

I think that Donald Hall was an institution, like a university, not the name of a husband. You don't want to be married to the *name* of a poet, either. Students called me Don, late '60s, early '70s. When we first moved to New Hampshire we were driving in Maine. There's a town called Perkins Cove and Jane saw 'Perkins Drugstore', 'Perkins' this and 'Perkins' that. She laughed and said, 'This fellow Perkins must be quite a fellow.' She started calling me Perkins from that day. She would always use Perkins if she was reproaching me. 'Perkins, dim your lights.' But she also used it affectionately. I loved it.

I had the idea that there was a Perkins in your family background?

I can't remember one. I might well have used it as a changed name in *The One Day.* I may have put Perkins's Store somewhere. I've just done a book of essays called *Principle Products of Portugal* – it's a miscellaneous collection. Jane always used to call me 'Perkins P. Perkins, Peripatetic Purveyor of Prose and Poetry,' so I continued the Ps.

What else are you writing now?

Lately, I've been writing some rhymed poems. Of course, I grew up writing rhymed poems. These are quite different. When Bayley reviewed *Without* he compared me to Thomas Hardy, thinking of Hardy's poems out of his wife's death. It pleased me because I love Hardy. I wondered why I had never tried to write that Hardy kind of stanza. I began to write a poem in which the lines varied and the rhymes but the second stanza matched the first and so on. I'd never done this before. The other night in Belfast I read three of these new things aloud. I'm fascinated now by doing this. Rhyming over and over again and making the rhyme natural, not forced. The metre's no problem, nor moving from pentameter to dimeter to trimeter. The rhyming is more of a problem but fascinating. I find it seems easier than free verse. It's easier to frame what you are doing, to know what you're doing.

You know more easily when you're finished.

The click of the box. Certainly. My favourite two lines in these poems are a couplet:

> Wool squares she used to knit
> While I sat opposite.

Are these rhymed poems about Jane?

I've been trying to write some that are *not*. There are also some free verse erotic poems, not about Jane. But there's an absolute connection even there. In my nightmares she left me for another man. I've a poem called 'Ardor' which begins with Jane's death and talks about other women and ends up saying:

> Lust is grief
> that has turned over in bed
> to look the other way.

That's how the erotic poems are related to her death. 'Ardor' offended some people when it came out in *The New Yorker*. The three in rhyme that I read in Belfast recently, though, are all directly to do with Jane. One is about her garden, and has a refrain: *'let it go, let it go':*

76

I let her garden go.
          let it go, let it go
How can I watch the hummingbird
          Hover to sip
          With its beak's tip
The purple bee balm – whirring as we heard
          It years ago?

Are the neo-formalists a hoax?

Most of them can count up to ten. One or two of them I have taught to scan. One of them suggested Frost didn't scan, as of course he did. I took a look at the lines he cited, and noticed Frost doing something fairly audacious. Something Wordsworth would not have done, I think: two medial inversions in a row. My friend did not hear the lines as scannable. Milton did it.

There was an anthology which purported to be contemporary poetry in metrics. They printed two poems of mine which were, in fact, free verse. Stupidly I let them do it. I wrote to the guy who edited it and said they were in free verse. He replied saying, 'That's what you think.' That amused me so much that I let him do it. There were other poems in the book that were also in free verse. One younger formalist said to me, 'Anything *is* pentameter that *looks* like pentameter.'

I don't know if something like it happens in the States but in the '80s here there was a widespread habit of people writing three lines, or two lines, as stanzas, stopping wherever, irrespective of rhythm, meaning, syntax, punctuation, 'stanza' end or expressive shaping. It was a sort of metrication by format, a purely visual shape or typographical metrics.

Speaking of hoaxes: do you know a poem of mine called 'Another Elegy, for William Trout'? In *The Museum of Clear Ideas?* It's for a dead poet of my generation called William Trout, a pure invention. I have a mad biographical note about him which is 'quoted' from *The Norton Book of Contemporary Verse,* which does not exist. This poem began as an elegy for James Wright. Then I worked in, oh, Ray Carver and John Logan, other drunks, but also Galway Kinnell and Bly and myself. It was a way of assembling my generation. I didn't think anybody would be taken in by the invention, but apparently people went into bookshops asking for the poems of William Trout. I love making fake epigraphs too. In *The One Day* I have a long one purporting to translate eighteenth-century French prose by the Abbé Michel de Bourdeille. Remember him? Yeats, 'The Three Bushes'. Yeats made him up, and I stole the lie from Yeats. I thought people would notice but nobody did. Some reviewer actually referred learnedly to my quoting from the Abbé. I put fake notes at the back of *The Old Life*. – There's a scathing review of me, by someone in 'The Inward Review of Books', and an interview with me ... Ah, it's fun.

I gather you once sent off the work of friends who were too nervous to submit it themselves.

That was a hoax I enjoyed. Harmless. I mean to say it never hurt anybody. I invented a name, had stationery made, got a post-office box in a different town. I didn't send out under my own name because some editors would have thought, 'Hall's trying to throw his weight around.' I sent poems to *The New Yorker*, *Poetry* and all sorts of places. *The New Yorker* took three, *Poetry* more. Sending out other people's poems helped me *not* to send out my own, to hold back. There was one editor, who has considerable dislike for me, who seemed quite to like the man who was sending in these poems. Only one editor saw through it all. He told me and I asked him to shut up about it. I can't remember how he twigged. De Snodgrass has used pseudonyms and dodges, too.

Yes, but one was because of the closeness of the material to his family.

S. S. Gardons's poems were written about his mother, father, a sister – and they were poems that would have caused pain. Eventually he could print them under his own name. – The best hoax, of course, was the Ern Malley affair.

But to go back to metrics for a moment: are they studied now in writing courses?

Some places do, but many don't. A course on the craft of verse might get to, touch on it. When I first taught at Michigan I would get them to write in metre but when the '60s hit hard, metrical exercises destroyed the class. It's a pity. You need to know or hear metre for reading most English verse. Before we knew each other, Jane took a big class of mine which was an introduction to poetry for non-English majors. She was a French major then. I gave a metrical lecture, an hour and a half, working with the notion of relative stress. At the end of the lecture a hand went up and someone asked, 'You mean something is *louder* than something else, not that it's *loud*?' That was Jane. We remembered it later.

Do you keep up with the younger generations? Are you interested in what they are doing, trying to do?

I try, but I feel less and less competent to read them. This is the case with most elderly poets. I remember Eberhart telling me when he was fifty that he could no longer tell the young apart from each other. Eliot, obviously, kept up.

Oh, I imagine he had a lot of advisers.

I'm not going to judge contests any more because I don't feel happy doing it. There are *some* quite young writers whose poems I do connect with. When I was twenty-five I felt I *knew* what was good and what was not. I was passionate about it. I'm not now. When it doesn't matter so much, it's time to stop. I'm sent lots of books. I keep track in magazines, see what strikes me – but without the old confidence.

I think it's possible to judge your own generation and what went before but what's younger is another thing.

I could judge for a while, helped by Jane. She was nineteen years younger than me. I could read the poets just younger than me: Mark Strand, Louise Glück, Charles Wright, Charles Simic. With Jane I could follow a little further.

One service you performed as an editor was to inaugurate The University of Michigan Press's series, Poets on Poetry. *Each volume has a poet talking about their own practice and the practice of others, and now, twenty years on, the list runs to something like sixty titles. Can you tell us about the series's genesis? Would I be right in thinking that you felt there was too little of this kind of talk going on back in the 1960s and 1970s, perhaps as a result of younger poets wishing to get away from the discursiveness of their New Critical forebears?*

Exactly. The poets of my generation were determined not to be known as critics, because the generations of Ransom and Tate, Warren and Jarrell, had frequently seemed more interested in criticism than poetry. However, my generation did interviews, and wrote the odd essay or review. These pieces were printed in fugitive magazines, and never collected into one place. I had the notion of the Poets on Poetry series, each collecting disparate pieces by one poet, and first proposed it to Harper and Row. Thank goodness they turned it down, because the first titles would have sold a few hundred copies and they would have ended it. I was in Ann Arbor, so I approached the University of Michigan Press. There are some terrible books in that series but in general it pleases me. It did what I wanted. After our series got started, other poets collected miscellaneous prose for their own publishers.

Yehuda Amichai, in an interview for The Paris Review, *said: 'I think it's natural for poets to become friends, but I also think, after a certain time, it's very difficult for poets to keep a friendship alive – for example, I've always felt that if two poets marry, the marriage has to be almost impossible.' You have been a rather obvious exception to Amichai's rule – some of your friendships with poets go back fifty years, and you were also happily married to a poet for over twenty – but would you accept that these relationships have been exceptions, exceptions that proved the general rule? And if so, to what do you think you owe your good fortune?*

Yes, I am an exception – although a couple of my oldest friendships have recently ended in estrangement. Jane and I did well together. It was helpful that we belonged to different generations. Her first book came out the year my sixth book came out, so our competition was not head to head. Living together, we kept clear boundaries. In the last five years we did many poetry readings together, going ABAB. Always the poet who begins, in a double reading, is the warm-up band. We scrupulously alternated being the warm-up band. In the house, we each knew that the other would never read a lying-about manuscript without being asked. We didn't interrupt each other working. If we met during work-time – in the kitchen getting another cup of coffee maybe – we would not even speak; I would pat her ass. We had so many things we cared about together, besides staring into each other's eyes, so many third things: poetry, of course, Eagle Pond, the church, baseball, our landscape. Even sex becomes a kind of third thing, after twenty-odd years: something purely erotic, without adventure or romance or sentimentality.

=

Tidying

A small mouse flitters across
the floor of the old parlour
and disappears among cartons.
On the carpet lie stacked
a thousand books,
acquired in excitement, now
given away unread. I find
a picture that we hung
over the sofa for ten years,
and discover another cache
of Jane's dresses and jackets.
Here's an album of snapshots
she took in China.

*

          I open a box
that emptied a bureau drawer
in my mother's Connecticut
attic, and an intact day
from nineteen-forty-two
leaps like a mouse surprised
eating a letter: a balsa
model of a Flying Fortress;
a ten-inch 78 of Connie
Boswell singing 'The Kerry
Dancers'; a verse play:
The Folly of Existence;
the unbearable photographs
of young parents who cannot
know what will happen.
Exposed, a discovered body
crumbles into motes
revolving in deadly air.

*

          By
wavery piles of tapes and CDs
near the TV, I find an electric
grinder, wedged in, labeled,
'To grind Indian spices *only.*'
Her underline. Why have I never
seen it, years after her death?

How did it get there? Maybe Jane
carried the grinder as the phone
rang, and set it down to hear
about bloodwork.

*

                    A friend
fills boxes of books to mail
to a Sioux reservation.
At a chest of drawers packed
with linen, she stands beside me
holding a trash bag. I lift
pillowcases, sheets, napkins,
doilies, and tablecloths,
and shake out weightless dry
housefly carcasses. Most
of the fabric is rotten or holey
or blood-stained. Sometimes
she says, 'This one is hand
done. This one is old.' We keep
the pretty pieces, fancy work
of farm women who sat at night
underneath the parlour's
kerosene lamp, their busy fingers
scampering in the yellow light
as quick as mice.

*

                    To the dump
with Bing Crosby and Dinah Shore,
with my mother's unfinished
tatting and her Agatha Christies.
To the dump with my father's
colourless Kodachrome slides
of their cross-country trip
together. To the dump
with bundles of stained linen
and the gooseneck lamp Jane
wrote poems by. To the dump
with the baseball and its eaten-
away glove, with my father,
dead forty years, with my mother
who lasted until ninety, with
Jane, with generations of mice,
with me – tidying, opening
boxes, throwing so much away.

Bibliography

The editors wish to express their gratitude to Jack Kelleher, from whose *Donald Hall: A Bibliographical Checklist* the following is adapted. The *Checklist*, which features a foreword by Richard Wilbur, and includes commentary by Donald Hall, is due from Warwick Press of Easthampton, Massachusetts, in January 2000.

PRIMARY WORKS

POETRY

BOOKS

A Single Look: Poems, DH writing under the pseudonym of Rhadamanthus Gall; poems submitted for the Lloyd McKim Garrison Prize, Harvard 1951, 26p, p/b, on deposit at the Harvard University Archives, Cambridge, MA.

Donald Hall, eds. Michael Shanks and Oscar Mellor, The Fantasy Poets, no. 4, Oxford University Poetry Society, Oxford, 1952, 8p, p/b.

The Fantasy Poets, one copy printed and bound for DH by Oscar Mellor, Oxford University Poetry Society, Oxford, 1952, 64p, h/b; included are Fantasy Poets pamphlets nos. 1 - 8, of which no. 4 is *Donald Hall*.

Exile: the Newdigate prize poem, 1952, Fantasy Press, Swinford, Eynsham, Oxon., 1952, 7 p, p/b, privately printed for DH by Oscar Mellor.

To the Loud Wind, and other poems, The Harvard Advocate, Cambridge MA, 1955, 26p, p/b, with Pegasus Publication Series, 1:1, 1955.

Exiles and Marriages, Viking Press, NY, 1955, 118p, h/b.

The Dark Houses, Viking Press, NY, 1958, 63p, h/b.

A Roof of Tiger Lilies, André Deutsch, London, 1964, 63p, h/b; Viking, NY, 1964, h/b.

The Alligator Bride (poem), Ox Head Press, (Ox Head 6), Menomonie, WI, April - June 1968, 13p, p/b.

The Alligator Bride: Poems New and Selected, Harper & Row, NY, 1969, 95p, h/b + p/b.

The Yellow Room: Love Poems, Harper & Row, NY, 1971, 74p, h/b + p/b.

The Gentleman's Alphabet Book, with limericks by DH, drawings by Harvey Kornberg, Dutton, NY, 1972, 61p, h/b.

A Blue Wing Tilts at the Edge of the Sea: Selected Poems, 1964-1974, Secker and Warburg, London, 1975, 62p, h/b + p/b.

Kicking the Leaves: a Poem in Seven Parts, with an engraving by Reynolds Stone, Perishable Press, Mt. Horeb, WI, 1975, 10 leaves, limited edition.

The Town of Hill, D. R. Godine, (A Godine Poetry Chapbook, Second Series), Boston, MA, 1975, 44p, h/b.

Kicking the Leaves, Harper and Row, NY, 1978, 58 p, h/b + p/b; Secker & Warburg, London, 1979, 47 p, h/b.

O Cheese (poem), The King Library Press, 1979, 8p.

The Toy Bone, BOA Editions, Brockport, NY, 1979, 14p, h/b + p/b.

The Twelve Seasons (poem), with hand-coloured illustration by Timothy Engelland, Deerfield Press, Deerfield, MA; Gallery Press, Dublin, Ireland, 1983, 11p, h/b.

Brief Lives: Seven Epigrams, William B. Ewert, Concord, MA, 1983, 12 leaves, h/b + p/b.

Couplet — Old Timer's Day, Fenway Park, 1 May 1982 (poem), Tom Clark, Berkeley, CA, 1984, 15p, p/b, a handmade book, with a drawing of Ted Williams on the cover, hand-coloured by Tom Clark, produced in an edition of one.

Great Day in the Cows' House (poem), with photographs by T.S. Bronson, Ives Street Press, Mt Carmel, CT, 1984, 1 folded leaf.

The Happy Man, Random House, NY, 1986, 79p, h/b + p/b; Secker & Warburg, London, 1986, p/b.

The One Day: a Poem in Three Parts, with a jacket illustration by Thomas W. Nason, Ticknor & Fields, NY, 1988, 69p, h/b + p/b.

Four Stories, Ives Street Press, Sweden, ME, 1989, 34p, h/b, limited edition.

Old and New Poems, with a jacket illustration by Michael McCurdy, Ticknor & Fields, NY, 1990, 244p, h/b + p/b.

The One Day and Poems, 1947-1990, Carcanet Press Ltd., Manchester, UK, 1991, 296p, h/b.

Daylilies on the Hill (poem), with two woodcut illustrations by Mary Azarian, William B. Ewert, Concord, NH, 1992, 24p, h/b + p/b, signed limited edition.

The Museum of Clear Ideas, Ticknor & Fields, NY, 1993, 120p, h/b + p/b.

Old and New Poems, EWP/Rajkamal Electric Press, New Delhi, India, 1993, 244p, p/b, printed in honour of the 1993 visit to India by DH and Jane Kenyon.

Apples and Peaches, with a cover illustration by Bayard Massey, R. L. Barth, Edgewood, KY, 1995, 16p, p/b.

Den enda dagen: endikt i tre delar, a translation into Swedish of *The One Day: A Poem in Three Parts* by Stewe Claeson, with cover illustration by Thomas W. Nason, Ellerstroms, Tryck Grahns, Lund, Sweden, 1995, 79p, p/b.

Ric's Progress (poem), with drawings by Carol J. Blinn, Warwick Press, Easthampton, MA, 1996, 22p, h/b, signed limited edition.

The Old Life, Houghton Mifflin, Boston, MA, 1996, 134p, h/b; Mariner Books, 1997, p/b.

Without, Houghton Mifflin, NY, 1998, 81p, h/b & p/b.

Winter Poems from Eagle Pond, with illustrations by Barry Moser and others, Wings Press, San Antonio, TX, 1999, limited to 700 copies, of which 300 are numbered and signed by DH.

BROADSIDES

'Stories' (poem), in *Ligature '68,* N. Schulson and E. Hearne, Madison Park Press, Chicago,1968.

'Jane at Pigall's' (poem), The Red Hanrahan Press, Highland Park, MI, 1973.

'Mouth' (poem), Arts Workshop Press, East Lansing, MI, 1973, limited to 350 copies, of which the first 30 are numbered and signed by DH.

'Valentine' (poem), privately printed, 1978, announcing the wedding of David Godine and Sylvia Davatz.

'On Reaching the Age of Two Hundred' (poem), The Poetry/Rare Books Collection, State University of New York, Buffalo, NY, 1979.

'My Son, My Executioner' (poem), in *Port Townsend Portfolio 1980,* Copper Canyon Press, Port Townsend, WA, 1980.

'Ox Cart Man' (poem), with calligraphy and illustration by Douglas Strickler, Friends of U.N.H. Library, Durham, NH, 1983, limited to 100 copies, of which 30 are numbered and signed by DH.

'Birch Maple Ash' (poem), in *Seven Holiday Greetings for 1985,* from William B. Ewert, publisher, William B. Ewert, Concord, NH, 1985.

'Carol' (poem), with woodcut illustration by J.J. Lankes, William B. Ewert, Concord, NH, 1988, limited to 25 copies signed by DH.

'Stoves and Kettles' (poem), William B. Ewert, Concord, NH, 1990, 36 numbered copies printed on special paper and signed by DH.

'Ox Cart Man' (poem), in *Broadside series number 1*, Engdahl Typography, Vineburg, CA, 1990.

'In November/In Advent Waiting' (poem), William B. Ewert, Concord, NH, 1991, 36 numbered copies signed by DH.

'Old Roses' (poem), with woodcut hand-coloured illustration by Mary Azarian, William B. Ewert, Corncord, MA, 1992, 50 copies, signed by DH and the illustrator.

'Moon Clock' (poem), Powell's Books, Portland, OR, 1992.

'Mount Kearsarge Shines' (poem), with calligraphy and illustration by R.P.Hale, William B. Ewert, Concord, NH, 1993, limited to 350 copies, of which 30 are numbered, and 10 are signed by DH and the illustrator.

'Elbows' (poem), with illustration by Karla Elling, Mummy Mountain Press, 1993, 150 copies signed by DH and the illustrator.

'Poetry: The Unsayable Said' (lines from an essay), Copper Canyon Press, Port Townsend, WA, 1993.

'Blue' (poem), with woodcut illustration by Mary Azarian, William B. Ewert, Concord, NH, 1994, 40 numbered copies signed by DH and the illustrator.

'Surface' (poem), with calligraphy and illustration by R.P.Hale, William B. Ewert, Concord, NH, 1995, 150 numbered copies signed by DH and the illustrator.

'The Pageant' (poem), with relief engraving illustration by Barry Moser, William B. Ewert, Concord, NH, 1995, 75 numbered copies, designed by John Kristensen, signed by DH and the illustrator.

'Weeds and Peonies' (poem), M. Schorr, 1996, Andover, MA, 25 copies printed in honour of the Andover memorial reading for Jane Kenyon held in May 1996.

'The Hunters' (poem), with artwork by Valia Oliver, White Pine Press Signature Editions, Fredonia, NY, 1996, 50 numbered copies signed by DH and the artist.

'On New Canada Road' (poem), with calligraphy and illustration by R. P. Hale, William B. Ewert, Concord, NH, 1997, 450 copies, of which 40 are numbered and signed by DH and the calligrapher.

'Ardor' (poem), Wolfe Editions, Portland, ME, 1998, 150 numbered copies, signed by DH.

'Weeds and Peonies' (poem), with calligraphy and illustration by R. P. Hale, William B. Ewert, Concord, NH,1998, limited to 450 copies, of which 40 are signed by DH and the calligrapher.

Cards and Postcards

'Breasts' (poem) (postcard), The Red Hanrahan Press, Highland Park, MI, 1973.

'Measure' (holiday card), with woodcut illustration by J. J. Lankes, William B. Ewert, Concord, NH, 1983, limited to 436 copies, of which 36 are numbered and signed by DH.

'December Stove' (poem) (holiday card), illustrated by Jane Banquer Burnham, William B. Ewert, Concord, NH, 1984, limited to 536 copies, of which 36 are numbered and signed by the DH.

'Birch Maple Ash' (poem) (holiday card), with calligraphy and illustration by R.P.Hale, William B. Ewert, Concord, NH, 1985, limited to 336 copies, of which 36 are numbered and signed by DH.

'The Onset' (holiday card), with calligraphy and illustration by R. P. Hale, William B. Ewert, Concord, NH, 1986, limited to 330 copies, of which 26 lettered and 4 *ad personam* copies are specially bound and signed by the DH.

'Carol' (poem) (holiday card), with woodcut illustration by J. J. Lankes, William B. Ewert, Concord, NH, 1988, limited to 436 copies, of which 26 lettered and 10 *ad personam* copies are signed by DH.

'Moon Clock' (poem) (holiday card), with calligraphy and illustration by R.P.Hale, William B. Ewert, Concord, NH, 1989, limited to 436 copies, of which 26 lettered and 10 *ad personam* copies are signed by DH.

'Stoves and Kettles' (poem) (holiday card), William B. Ewert, Concord, NH, 1990, limited to 286 copies, of which 36, on special paper, are signed by DH and issued as a broadside.

'In November / In Advent Waiting' (poem) (holiday card), William B. Ewert, Concord, NH, 1991, limited to 336 copies, of which 36, printed on Umbria, are signed by DH and issued as a broadside.

'Old Roses' (poem) (holiday card), with woodcut illustration, hand-coloured by Mary Azarian, William B. Ewert, Concord, NH, 1992, limited to 450, of which 50, printed on Rives BFK, are signed by DH and the illustrator and issued as a broadside.

(From) 'Baseball' (poem) (publicity postcard), Ticknor & Fields, NY, 1993.

'Mount Kearsarge Shines' (poem) (holiday card), with calligraphy and illustration by R. P. Hale, William B. Ewert, Concord, NH, 1993, limited to 310 copies, signed by DH.

'A Carol' (poem) (holiday card), Town and Country Reprographics, Concord, NH, 1993, limited to 300 copies.

'Blue' (poem) (holiday card), with woodcut illustration by Mary Azarian, William B. Ewert, Concord, NH, 1994, limited to 400 copies, of which 40 are signed by DH and the artist and issued as a broadside.

'The Pageant' (poem) (holiday card), with relief engraving by Barry Moser, William B. Ewert, Concord, NH, 1995, limited to 650 copies, of which 75, printed on special paper are signed by DH and the artist and issued as a broadside.

'Apples and Peaches' (poem) (postcard), Davis, CA (*An Epigrammatist Postcard*), 1995.

'The Absence' (poem) (postcard), Davis, CA (*An Epigrammatist Postcard*), 1995.

'Eagle Pond Epigrams' (card), with portrait of DH by David Oliveira, Mille Grazie Press, 1995.

'On New Canada Road' (poem) (holiday card), with calligraphy and illustration by R. P. Hale, William B. Ewert, Concord, NH, 1997, limited to 450 copies, of which 40 numbered copies, printed on special paper, are signed by DH and the calligrapher.

'Weeds and Peonies' (poem) (holiday card), with calligraphy and illustration by R. P. Hale, William B. Ewert, Concord, NH, 1998, limited to 450 copies, of which 40 are signed by DH and the calligrapher.

PROSE

BOOKS

The Challenge of the War to American Youth: an Address by Donald A. Hall, Jr. Freshman, Hamden High School, 1943, 8p, p/b.

Yeats' Stylistic Development as Seen Through a Consideration of His Published Revisions of
  'The Rose', 50p, p/b, DH's BA Hons senior thesis, Harvard University, Cambridge,
  MA, 1951, on deposit at the Harvard University Archives, Cambridge, MA.
String Too Short to be Saved, illustrated by Mimi Korach, Viking, NY, 1961; André Deutsch,
  London, 1962, 143p, h/b; Country Book Club, London, 1963, 141p, h/b.
Henry Moore: the Life and Work of a Great Sculptor, Harper & Row, NY; Victor Gollancz,
  London, 1966, 182p, h/b.
Marianne Moore: the Cage and the Animal, Pegasus (Pegasus American Authors), NY, 1970,
  199 p, h/b.
As the Eye Moves .... a Sculpture by Henry Moore, words by DH, photographs by David
  Finn, Abrams, NY, 1970, 161p, h/b.
Writing Well, Little, Brown, Boston, MA, 1973, 324p, p/b.
Teaching Writing Well, with D. L. Emblen, Little, Brown, Boston, MA, 1973, 144p, p/b.
Goatfoot, Milktongue, Twinbird, Oberlin College, Oberlin, OH, 1973.
Playing Around: The Million-Dollar Infield Goes to Florida, with others, and with photos by
  Bob Adelman, and an introduction by Dock Ellis, Little, Brown, Boston, MA, 1974,
  248p, h/b.
Dock Ellis in the Country of Baseball, with Dock Ellis, photographs by Jane Kenyon, Cow-
  ard, McCann & Geoghegan, NY, 1976, 254p, h/b.
Writing Well, Little, Brown, Boston, MA, 1976, 388p, p/b, second edition.
*Remembering Poets: Reminiscences and Opinions: Dylan Thomas, Robert Frost, T. S. Eliot,
  Ezra Pound*, Harper & Row, NY, 1978, xv, 253p, h/b; Harper Colophon Edition,
  NY, 1979, p/b.
Goatfoot Milktongue Twinbird: Interviews, Essays, and Notes on Poetry, 1970-76, Univer-
  sity of Michigan Press (Poets on Poetry series), Ann Arbor, MI, 1978, 208p, p/b.
String Too Short to be Saved, with Illustrations by Mimi Korach, D.R.Godine (Nonpareil
  Books, 5), Boston, MA, 1979, 155p, h/b, second edition.
Writing Well, Little, Brown, Boston, MA, 1979, 416p, p/b, third edition.
To Keep Moving: Essays, 1959-1969, Hobart & William Smith Colleges Press, Geneva, NY,
  in association with *Seneca Review*, 1980, 175p, p/b.
String Too Short To Be Saved, G. K. Hall, Boston, MA, 1980, 297p, large print edition.
The Weather for Poetry: Essays, Reviews, and Notes on Poetry, 1977-81, University of Michi-
  gan Press (Poets on Poetry series), Ann Arbor, MI, 1982, 336p, p/b.
Writing Well, Little, Brown, Boston, MA, 1982, 435p, p/b, fourth edition.
Christmas Snow: a Story, with wood engravings by Randy Miller, privately printed by DH,
  Sant Bani Press, Tilton, New Hampshire, 1982, 19p, p/b, limited edition.
Fathers Playing Catch With Sons: Essays on Sport, with jacket illustration by Thomas Eakins,
  North Point Press, San Francisco, CA, 1985, 200p, p/b.
Writing Well, Little, Brown, Boston, MA, 1985, 473p, p/b, fifth edition.
Fathers Playing Catch With Sons: Essays on Sport, Dell Publishing Co., NY, 1986, 198p, p/
  b.
The Ideal Bakery: Stories, with jacket illustration by Ginny Crouch Stanford, North Point
  Press, San Francisco, CA, 1987, 141p, h/b.
Seasons at Eagle Pond, with illustrations by Thomas W. Nason, Ticknor & Fields, NY, 1987,
  87p, h/b + p/b.
Writing Well, Scott, Foresman, Glenview, IL,1988, 504p, p/b, sixth edition.
Poetry and Ambition: Essays, 1982-88, University of Michigan Press (Poets on Poetry Se-
  ries), Ann Arbor, MI, 1988, 207p, h/b + p/b.
The Ideal Bakery: Stories, Perennial Library, NY, 1988, 138p, p/b.
Dock Ellis in the Country of Baseball, with Dock Ellis, Simon & Schuster (Fireside Sports
  Classic), NY, 1989, 347p, p/b, second edition.

(From) *Seasons at Eagle Pond,* designed by Jerry Kelly and Earl Kallemeyn, Center for Book Arts, NY, 1989, 3p, p/b, one hundred copies, not for sale, reprinted by permission of Houghton Mifflin Co., at the Center for Book Arts, NY, December 9, 1989.

Here at Eagle Pond, with illustrations by Thomas W. Nason, Ticknor & Fields, NY, 1990, 143p, h/b + p/b.

Writing Well, with Sven Birkerts, HarperCollins, NY, 1991, 484p, student and teacher editions, p/b, seventh edition.

Their Ancient Glittering Eyes: Remembering Poets and More Poets: Robert Frost, Dylan Thomas, T.S. Eliot, Archibald MacLeish, Yvor Winters, Marianne Moore, Ezra Pound, Ticknor & Fields, NY, 1992, 348p, h/b; 1993, p/b.

Life Work, Beacon Press, Boston, 1993, 124p, h/b; 1994, p/b.

Poetry: the Unsayable Said: an Essay, Copper Canyon Press, Port Townsend, WA, 1993, 12p, p/b.

Life Work, Contemporary Large Print, Hampton, NH, 1994, 152p, h/b + p/b, large print edition.

Death to the Death of Poetry: Essays, Reviews, Notes, Interviews, University of Michigan Press (Poets on Poetry series), 1994, Ann Arbor, MI, 157p, h/b + p/b.

Writing Well, with Sven Birkerts, HarperCollins College Publishers, NY, 1994, 407p, p/b, eighth edition.

Principal Products of Portugal: Prose Pieces, Beacon Press, Boston, MA, 1995, 271p, h/b; 1996, p/b.

Writing Well, with Sven Birkerts, Longman, NY, 1998, 382p, p/b, ninth edition.

CHILDREN'S BOOKS

Andrew the Lion Farmer, illustrated by Jane Miller, F. Watts Inc., NY, 1959, 58p, h/b; illustrated by Ann Reason, Methuen and Co., Ltd, London, 1961, 47p, h/b; illustrated by Jane Miller, E. M. Hale/Cadmus Editions, Eau Claire, WI, 1964, 55p, h/b.

Riddle Rat, illustrated by Mort Gerberg, F. Warne, NY, 1977, 57p, h/b.

Ox Cart Man, illustrated by Barbara Cooney, Viking Press, NY, 1979; Macrae Books, London, 1980, 40p, h/b.

Ox Cart Man, illustrated by Barbara Cooney, Japanese translation by Kazuko Moki, Horupu Shuppan, Tokyo, 1980, 37p, h/b.

Quand le Fermier Se Rendait au Marche, illustrated by Barbara Cooney, French translation of *Ox Cart Man* by Catherine Deloraine, Flammarion, Paris, France, 1981, 40p, h/b + p/b.

Og Sa Blev Det Oktober, illustrated by Barbara Cooney, Danish translation of *Ox Cart Man* by Poul Steenstrup, Gyldendal, Copenhagen, Denmark, 1982, 40p, h/b.

Oxkarre-Mannen, illustrated by Barbara Cooney, Swedish translation of *Ox Cart Man* by Barbro Lindgren, Raben & Sjogren, Stockholm, Sweden, 1982, 40p, h/b.

Ox Cart Man, illustrated by Barbara Cooney, Puffin Books (Picture Puffins Series), NY, 1983, 40p, p/b.

The Man Who Lived Alone, illustrated by Mary Azarian, D.R. Godine, Boston, MA, 1984, 36p, h/b.

Ox Cart Man, Scholastic, NY, 1989, 40p.

I Am the Dog, I Am the Cat, illustrated by Barry Moser, Dial Books for Young Readers, NY, 1994, 32p, h/b; Scholastic/Trumpet Club, 1996, p/b.

The Farm Summer 1942, illustrated by Barry Moser, Dial Books, NY, 1994, 32p, h/b.

Lucy's Christmas, illustrated by Michael McCurdy, Browndeer Press, Harcourt Brace Jovanovich, San Diego, CA, 1994, 40p, h/b; Voyager Picture Books, 1998, p/b.

Lucy's Summer, illustrated by Michael McCurdy, Browndeer Press, Harcourt Brace Jovanovich, San Diego, CA, 1995, 40p, h/b; Voyager Picture Books, 1998, p/b.

Old Home Day, illlustrated by Emily Arnold McCully, Browndeer Press, San Diego, CA, 1996, 48p, h/b.

When Willard Met Babe Ruth, illustrated by Barry Moser, Browndeer Press, San Diego, CA, 1996, 41p, h/b.

Ox Cart Man, illustrated by Barbara Cooney, Korean translation, BIR Publishing Co., Ltd., Korea, 1997, 40p, h/b + p/b.

The Milkman's Boy, illustrations by Greg Shed, Walker and Co., NY, 1997, 32p, h/b.

The Man Who Lived Alone, illustrated by Mary Azarian, D. R. Godine, Jaffrey, NH, 1998, 36p, p/b.

TRANSLATIONS

'Sixth Ode', Third Book, Horace, translated by DH under the pseudonym of P. M. Lesbius, 4p, p/b, on deposit at Harvard University Archives, Cambridge, MA.

PLAYS

The Bone Ring (verse play), Story Line Press, Santa Cruz, CA, 1987, 57p, h/b & p/b.

THEATRICAL PERFORMANCES

The Minstrel's Progress, music by Howard Brown, adapted from Eleanor Farjeon's children's book, *Martin Pippin in the Apple Orchard,* Stokes, 1922, performed at Poets' Theater, Harvard University, Cambridge, MA, Spring, 1951, for one night.

An Evening's Frost, first performed, 1964, Professional Theater Program, University of Michigan, Ann Arbor, MI; Theatre de Lys, NYC, 10.11.65 through to early 1966; toured the U.S. during 1967; staged by the American Conservatory Theater on the West Coast in 1968; further productions: 1981, 1982.

Bread and Roses, music by William Bolcom, first produced at the Power Center, Ann Arbor, MI, February 1975.

Ragged Mountain Elegies, directed by Charles Morey, performed by the Peterborough Players, 17.8.83 - 31.8.83, Peterborough, N.H.

The Bone Ring, directed by Kent Paul, performed at Theater of the Open Eye, NYC, 1.2.86 - 25.2.86; directed by Robert Shea for the New Art Theatre, New Hampshire Institute of Art, Manchester, NH, 12.3.98 - 15.3.98.

CONTRIBUTOR

'Blueberry Picking' (poem), in *Trails: A Literary Magazine of the Outdoors*, 14:1, Fall 1945, pp. 16, ed. Fred Lape, Esperance, N. Y.

'New England November' (poem), in *American Writing Today: its Independence and Vigour*, Special Number of *The Times Literary Supplement*, September 17, 1954, pp. 581 - 600.

'The New Poetry: Notes on the Past Fifteen Years in America' (essay), in *New World Writing: 7th Mentor Selection*, New American Library, NY, April 1955, 256p, p/b, pp. 231 - 247.

'The Art of Poetry, I: T. S. Eliot' (interview with Eliot), *The Paris Review*, 21, Spring-Summer 1959, pp. 47 - 70.

Wolgamot Interstice (poems), with W.D. Snodgrass and X.J. Kennedy, ed. D. C. Hope, Burning Deck, Ann Arbor, MI, 1961, 51p, p/b.

'The Art of Poetry, IV: Marianne Moore' (interview with Moore), *The Paris Review*, 26, 1961, pp. 40-66.

'A Day on Ragged' (short story), in *Best American Short Stories, 1962*, ed. Martha Foley and David Burnett, Houghton Mifflin, Boston, MA, 1962, 436p, h/b, pp. 181 - 199.

The Rock, Rebecca Richmond, with an appreciation by DH, Chautauqua Sandwich Poets, Chautauqua, NY, 1962, 58p, p/b.

Poetry in Crystal (interpretations in crystal of thirty-one new poems by contemporary American poets, including DH, Steuben Glass, NY, 1963, 86p, h/b; also limited edition of 250 numbered copies.

Poet's Choice, eds. Paul Engle and Joseph Langland, The Dial Press, NY, 1962, 303p, h/b.

Tess of the D'Urbervilles: a Pure Woman, Thomas Hardy, with an afterword by DH, New American Library (A Signet Classic), NY, 1964; latest edition, 1997, 35th printing; revised and updated bibliography, c.1980.

Washington Square, Henry James, with an afterword by DH, New American Library (A Signet Classic), NY, 1964, 192p, p/b; latest edition, 1997, 19th printing; revised and updated bibliography, c.1979.

'Spider Head' (poem), in *Of Poetry and Power: Poems Occasioned by the Presidency and by the Death of John F. Kennedy*, ed. and with an introduction by Erwin A. Glikes and Paul Schwaber, Basic Books, NY, 1964, 155p, h/b.

Hard Road Nowhere (poems), Robert Stevens Bronson, ed. George Abbott White, with an introduction by DH, Generation (Generation new poet series, 3), Ann Arbor, MI, 1965, 80p, h/b.

The Faber Book of Modern Verse, ed. Michael Roberts, Faber & Faber, London, 1965, 416p, h/b; third edition revised and with a new supplement of poems chosen and introduced by DH.

Writers at Work: The Paris Review Interviews, Second Series, prepared by George Plimpton, with an introduction by Van Wyck Brooks, Viking (Compass Books), NY,1965, 368p, p/b; includes DH's interviews with T. S. Eliot, Marianne Moore, and Ezra Pound.

Poems for Young Readers: Selections from Their Own Writing by Poets Attending the Houston Festival of Contemporary Poetry, National Council of Teachers of English, Houston, TX, 1966, 70p, p/b.

Laurel, Archaic, Rude (a collection of poems presented to Yvor Winters on his retirement by the Stanford English Department), Department of English, Stanford University, Stanford, California, 33p, h/b ; 300 numbered copies.

'The Inward Muse' (essay), in *The Poet as Critic*, ed. Frederick P. W. McDowell, Northwestern University Press, Evanston, IL, 1967, 113p, h/b.

'The Village Fish' (poem), in *Where is Vietnam? American Poets Respond*, ed. Walter Lowenfels, Anchor Books, Garden City, NY, 1967, 160p, p/b.

'Robert Lowell' (essay), in *Contemporary Poets of the English Language*, ed. Rosalie Murphy, St. James Press, NY, 1970, 1243p, h/b.

War, War, War (poems), Pierrott, Iowa City, IA, 1968, 8p, p/b.

Contemporary Poetry in America, ed. Miller Williams, Random House, NY,1973,189p, p/b.

'"Oh," said Kate, "I do love the sound of tennis balls!"' (poem) (postcard), in *Cold Mountain Press Poetry Post Card*, Series I, Cold Mountain Press, Austin, TX, 1973.

The World of Leon (poems), by Larry Fagin, Ted Berrigan and Ron Padgett, writing under the pseudonym, Leon, introduction by DH, *Big Sky* (# 7), Bolinas, CA , 1974, 48p, p/b.

The Third Coast: Contemporary Michigan Poetry, eds. Conrad Hilberry and others, Wayne State University Press, Detroit, MI, 1976, 296p, h/b + p/b.

Good Company - Poets at Michigan, ed. and with photographs by Jeanne Rockwell, introduction by Sheridan Baker, Noon Rock, Ann Arbor, 1977, 70p, p/b.

Fifty Contemporary Poets: the Creative Process, ed. Alberta T. Turner, McKay, NY, 1977, 355p, h/b + p/b.

Job Speaks: Interpreted from the Original Hebrew Book of Job, David Rosenberg, foreword by DH, Harper & Row, NY, 1977, 101p, h/b.

'Recessional' (poem), in *First Flowering: The Best of the Harvard Advocate*, ed. Richard M. Smoley, Addison-Wesley Publishing Co., Reading, MA, 1977, 335p, h/b.

'Passage' (poem) [postcard], illustrated by Ann Mikolowski, in *The Alternative Press*, 8, Alternative Press, 1978, Grindstone City, MI.

The Face of Poetry: 101 Poets in Two Significant Decades – the 60s & the 70s, eds. LaVerne Harrell Clark and Mary MacArthur, Heidelberg Graphics, Chico, CA,1979, 302 p, h/b.

Baseball Diamonds: Tales, Traces, Visions and Voodoo from a Native American Rite, ed. Kevin Kerrane and Richard Grussinge, Anchor/Doubleday, NY, 1980, 419p, p/b.

'The Internal Cape' (essay), in *Richard Eberhart: A Celebration, New England Review*, Kenyon Hill Publications, Hanover, NH, 1980, 73p, p/b.

'Poetry Food' (essay), in *Of Solitude and Silence: Writings on Robert Bly*, eds. Richard Jones and Kate Daniels, Beacon Press, Boston, MA, 1981, 278p, h/b + p/b.

New Hampshire Literature: a Sampler, ed. Robert C. Gilmore, Published for the University of New Hampshire by University Press of New England, Hanover, NH, 1981, 340p, h/b + p/b.

Poetry Comics!: a Cartooniverse of Poems, Dave Morice, Simon & Schuster, NY, 1982, 186p, h/b + p/b.

Birds, Beasts and the Third Thing: Poems by D. H. Lawrence, selected and illustrated by Alice and Martin Provensen, with an introduction by DH, Viking, NY, 1982, 40p, h/b.

Poetspeak: in their work, about their work: a selection, Paul B. Janeczko, Bradbury Press, Scarsdale, NY, 1983; Collier, NY, 1991, 238p, p/b.

Two Poems, DH and Robert Bly, Story Line Press, 1984, 4p, p/b.

Robert Bly: When Sleepers Awake, ed. Joyce Peseroff, University of Michigan Press, Ann Arbor, NY, 1984, 345p, h/b + p/b.

45 Contemporary Poems : the Creative Process, ed. Alberta Turner, Longman, NY, 1985, 246p, p/b.

Singular Voices : American Poetry Today, ed. Stephen Berg, Avon, NY, 1985, 326p, p/b.

'Winter' (essay), published on the occasion of the exhibition, *Winter*, 1.2.86 - 16.3.86, Hood Museum of Art, Dartmouth College, Hanover, NH, Hood Museum of Art, Dartmouth College, Hanover NH, distributed by University Press of New England, 1986, 138p, h/b + p/b.

'Christmas Snow: A Story', in *American Christmas: a Sampler of Contemporary Stories & Poems* , ed. Jane B. Hill, Peachtree Publishers, Atlanta, GA, 1986. 300p, h/b.

The Poetry of Geoffrey Hill, Henry Hart, with an introduction by DH, Southern Illinois University Press, Carbondale Il, 1986, 305p, h/b.

Valentino's Hair, Yvonne Sapia, poems selected and introduced by DH, Northeastern University Press, Boston, MA, 1987, 67p, p/b.

'English C, 1947' (essay), in *John Ciardi: Measure of a Man*, ed. Vince Clemente, University of Arkansas Press, Fayettesville, AK, 1987, 246p, h/b + p/b.

'Shapes of the Game Forever' (essay), in *Diamonds are Forever: Artists and Writers on Baseball*, ed. Peter H. Gordon with Sydney Waller and Paul Weinman, and an introduction by DH, Chronicle Books, San Francisco, CA, 1987, 166p, h/b + p/b.

The Best American Poetry 1988, ed. John Ashbery, Scribner, NY, 1988, 249p, h/b + p/b.

'A Ballad of the Republic' (essay), in *Casey at the Bat*, Ernest Lawrence Thayer, Illustrated by Barry Moser; afterword by DH, D. R. Godine, Boston, MA, 1988, 32p, h/b + p/b.

'Uncharted Waters' (essay), in *On Louis Simpson: Depths Beyond Happiness*, ed. Hank Lazer, University of Michigan Press, Ann Arbor, MI,1988, 398p, h/b + p/b.

'New England' (essay), in *Discover America! A Scenic Tour of the Fifty States*, National Geographic Society, Washington, DC., 1989, 336p, h/b.

The Best American Poetry 1989, ed. and with an introduction by Donald Hall, Scribner, NY, 1989, 293p, h/b + p/b.

Poets At Work: The Paris Review Interviews, ed. George Plimpton, with an introduction by DH, Penguin, NY, h/b; Viking, NY, p/b, 1989.

'Philip Larkin, 1922 - 1985' (essay), in *Philip Larkin: the Man and His Work*, ed. Dale Salwak,University of Iowa Press, Iowa City, IA, 1989, xviii, 184p, h/b.

Ox Cart Man (poem) (postcard), in *Zoland Books Poetry Postcard Collection*, ed. Roland Pease, Zoland Books, Cambridge, MA, 1989, 20p, p/b.

'Old Roses and Birdsong' (essay), in *Summer*, ed. Alice Gordon and Vincent Virga, Addison-Wesley Publishing Co., Reading, MA, 1990, 252p, h/b.

New England's Disastrous Weather, ed. Benjamin Watson, with foreword by DH, Yankee Books, Camden, ME, 1990, 228p, h/b.

Eighty Acres: Elegy for a Family Farm, Ronald Jager, with a foreword by DH, Beacon Press, Boston, MA, 1990, 257p, h/b + p/b.

'October's Shortstop' (essay), in *The Ol' Ball Game: a Collection of Baseball Characters and Moments Worth Remembering*, Stackpole Books, Harrisburg, PA, 1990, 178p, h/b.

The Best American Poetry 1990, ed. Jorie Graham, Collier Books, NY, 1990.

Above the River: The Complete Poems, James Wright, with an introduction by DH, Farrar, Straus and Giroux, NY; University Press of New England, Middletown, CT, 1990, 387p, h/b + p/b.

Our Other Voices: Nine Poets Speaking, ed. John Wheatcroft, Bucknell University Press, Lewisburg,1991, 217p, h/b.

The Essential Marvell, selected and with an introduction by DH, Ecco (*The Essential Poets*, 15), Hopewell, NJ, 1991, 119p, p/b.

The Glass House: the Life of Theodore Roethke, Allan Seager, with an Introduction by DH, University of Michigan Press, Ann Arbor, MI, 1991, 301p, h/b + p/b.

'That Swing' (essay), in *Ted Williams: a Portrait in Words and Pictures*, ed. Dick Johnson, Walker and Co., NY, 1991, 225p, h/b.

The Forgotten Language: Contemporary Poets and Nature, ed. Christopher Merrill, Peregrine Smith Books, Salt Lake City, UT, 1991, 176 p, p/b.

Hummers, Knucklers, and Slow Curves: Contemporary Baseball Poems, ed. Don Johnson, with a foreword by W. P. Kinsella, University of Illinois Press, Urbana, IL, 1991, 130 p, h/b + p/b.

'Last Train from Madrid' (essay), in *The Movie That Changed My Life*, ed. David Rosenberg, Viking, NY, 1991, 304 p, h/b.

Portraits of Trees: Exhibition of Photographs by Tom Zetterstrom, with text by DH, Bates College Museum of Art, Lewiston, ME, 1991.

Taking Note: from Poets' Notebooks, ed. Stephen Kuusisto et al, Hobart and William Smith Colleges Press, Geneva, NY, 1991, 244 p, p/b.

The Best American Poetry 1991, ed. Mark Strand, Scribner, NY, 1991, 326 p, h/b + p/b.

Wendell Berry, ed. Paul Merchant, Confluence Press, Lewsiton, ID,1991, 223 p, h/b & p/b.

'Haying, a Horse, and a Hired Man' (story), in *Late Harvest: Rural American Writing*, ed. David R. Pichaske, Paragon House, NY, 1992, 452 p, h/b.

'Young Bly' (essay), in *Critical Essays on Robert Bly*, ed. William V. Davis, G. K. Hall, NY, 1992, 304 p, h/b.

'Art and Its Enemies' (essay), in *Corporal Politics* (exhibition catalog), M.I.T. List Visual Arts Center, Cambridge, MA, 1992, 72 p, p/b.

'An Arc of Generations' (essay), in *Fathers and Sons: An Anthology*, ed. David Seybold, Grove Weidenfeld, NY, 1992, 203 p, h/b; Atlantic Monthly Press, 1995, p/b.

The Best American Poetry 1992, ed. Charles Simic, Scribner, NY, 1992, 263 p, h/b + p/b.

'A Friendship' (essay), in *Walking Swiftly: Writings in Honor of Robert Bly*, ed. Thomas R. Smith, Ally Press, St Paul, MN, 1992, 287 p, h/b; HarperPerennial, 1993, p/b.

A Piece of Work: Five Writers Discuss Their Revisions, ed. Jay Woodruff, University of Iowa Press, Iowa City, IA, 1993, 273 p, h/b + p/b.

'Seasoned Wood' (essay), in *The Poetry of W. D. Snodgrass: Everything Human*, ed. Stephen Haven, University of Michigan Press, Ann Arbor, MI, 1993, 315 p, h/b.

The Best American Poetry 1993, ed. Louise Gluck, Scribner, NY, 1993, 287 p, p/b.

'The Books Not Read, The Lines Not Written: a Poet Confronts His Mortality' (essay), in *The Best Writing on Writing*, ed. Jack Heffron, Story Press, Cincinnati, OH, 1994, 209 p, p/b.

The NPR Interviews 1994 , ed. and with an introduction by Robert Siegel, Houghton Mifflin Co., Boston, MA, 1994, 376 p, h/b + p/b.

The Essential Robinson, selected and with an introduction by DH, Ecco (*The Essential Poets, 19*), Hopewell, NJ, 1994, 145 p, p/b.

'Words for a Warrant'(poem), Jane Kenyon and DH, in *Town of Wilmot, New Hampshire: 1993 Annual Report*, 1994, 65 p, p/b.

The Best American Poetry 1994, ed. A. R. Ammons, Scribner, NY, 1994, 275 p, h/b + p/b.

The Poet's Notebook: Excerpts from the Notebooks of Contemporary American Poets, eds. Stephen Kuusisto, Deborah Tall & David Weiss, W.W. Norton & Co., NY and London, 1995, 306p, h/b.

The Language of Life: A Festival of Poets, Bill Moyers, Doubleday, NY, 1995, xx, 450 p, h/b; Main Street Books, 1996, p/b.

What Will Suffice: Contemporary American Poets on the Art of Poetry, ed. Christopher Buckley and Christopher Merrill, Gibbs Smith, Layton, UT, 1995, 180 p, p/b.

Where the Angels Come Toward Us: Select Essays, Reviews and Interviews, David St. John, White Pine Press, 1995, Fredonia, NY, 256 p, p/b.

'Life After Jane: an Essay', in Northeast: The Hartford [CT] Courant Sunday Magazine, August 27, 1995.

'The Accident ' (short story), in *The Ohio Review*, 55, 1996.

'Lake Paradise' (short story), in *Boulevard*, 11:1-2, 1996.

Drawing Your Own Conclusions: Government and the Arts: New Hampshire's Story, Rebecca L. Lawrence, with an introduction by DH, N.H. State Council on the Arts, Concord, NH, 1996, 53p, p/b.

Otherwise: New and Selected Poems, Jane Kenyon, with an afterword by DH, Graywolf Press, St Paul, MN, 1996, 230p, h/b + p/b.

'Poetry and Ambition' (essay) in *Written in Water, Written in Stone: Twenty Years of Poets on Poetry*, ed. Martin Lammon, with a foreword by David Lehman, The University of Michigan Press, Ann Arbor, MI, 1996, 288p, h/b + p/b.

The Best American Poetry 1996, ed. Adrienne Rich, Scribner, NY, 1996, 318p, h/b; Touchstone Books, NY, p/b.

'Winter' (essay), in *The Place Within: Portraits of the American Landscape by Twenty Contemporary Writers*, ed. Jodi Daynard, Morton, NY, 1997, 268p, h/b.

'From Willow Temple' (short story), in *The Best American Short Stories 1997*, ed. E. Annie Proulx, Houghton Mifflin, NY, 1997, 381p, h/b + p/b.

Briefly It Enters: a Cycle of Songs from Poems of Jane Kenyon, for voice and piano 1994-1996 (score), William Bolcom, E. B. Marks, Milwaukee, WI, 1997, 1 score, 35p, p/b, includes brief commentary by DH.

'Baseball and the Meaning of Life' (essay) in *The Complete Armchair Book of Baseball: An All-Star Lineup Celebrates America's National Pastime*, ed. John Thorn, Galahad Books, NY, 1997, 832p, h/b.

The Best American Poetry 1997, ed. James Tate, Scribner Poetry, NY, 1997, 269p, h/b + p/b.

The Best of the Best American Poetry 1988 - 1997, ed. Harold Bloom, series editor, David Lehman, Scribner Poetry, NY, 1998, 383p, h/b + p/b.

The Best American Poetry 1998, ed. John Hollander, Scribner Poetry, NY, 1998, 332p, p/b.

A Hundred White Daffodils: Essays, The Akhmatova Translations, Newspaper Columns,Notes, Interviews, and One Poem, Jane Kenyon, with an introduction by DH, Graywolf Press, St Paul, MN,1999, 229p, h/b.

'How to Peel a Poem'(discussion between DH, Charles Simic, Paul Muldoon, Cynthia Huntington and Heather McHugh of 'a poem he or she truly loves'), *Harper's*, September 1999, pp. 45-60.

The Best American Poetry 1999, ed. Robert Bly, Scribner Poetry, NY, 1999, 223p, h/b & p/b.

EDITIONS

The Harvard Advocate Anthology, Twayne Publishers, NY, 1950, 327p, with preface and introduction by DH.

Lotte Zurndorfer (poems), with Oscar Mellor, Oxford University Poetry Society (The Fantasy Poets, no. 9), Oxford, 1952, 8p, p/b.

Martin Seymour-Smith (poems), with Oscar Mellor, Oxford University Poetry Society (The Fantasy Poets, no. 10), Oxford, 1952, 8p, p/b.

Geoffrey Hill (poems), with Oscar Mellor, Oxford University Poetry Society (The Fantasy Poets, no. 11), Oxford, 1952, 8p, p/b.

Adrienne Cecile Rich (poems), with Oscar Mellor, Oxford University Poetry Society (The Fantasy Poets, no. 12), Oxford, 1952, 8p, p/b.

Michael Shanks (poems), with Oscar Mellor, Oxford University Poetry Society (The Fantasy Poets, no. 13), Oxford, 1952, 8p, p/b.

Michell Raper (poems), with Oscar Mellor, Oxford University Poetry Society (The Fantasy

Poets, no. 14), 1952, 8p, p/b.

A. *Alvarez* (poems), with Oscar Mellor, Oxford University Poetry Society (The Fantasy Poets, no. 15), 1952, 8p, p/b.

Thom Gunn (poems), with Oscar Mellor, Oxford University Poetry Society (The Fantasy Poets, no. 16), 1953, 8p p/b.

Anthony Thwaite (poems), with Oscar Mellor. Oxford University Poetry Society (The Fantasy Poets, no. 17), 1953, 8p, p/b.

Arthur Boyars (poems), with Oscar Mellor, Oxford University Poetry Society (The Fantasy Poets, no. 18), 1953, 8p, p/b.

Oxford Poetry 1953, with Geoffrey Hill, Fantasy Press, Swinford, Eynsham, Oxon, 1953.

New Poems (magazine), 1:1, autumn 1952 – 2:2, winter 1953, Fantasy Press, Swinford, Eynsham, Oxon.

New Poets of England and America, with Robert Pack and Louis Simpson, and with an introduction by Robert Frost, Meridian Books, NY, 1957, 351p, h/b + p/b.

Whittier (poems of John Greenleaf Whittier), selected, with an introduction and notes by DH, Dell Publishing Co (Laurel Poetry Series; Richard Wilbur, General Editor), NY, 1961, 159p, p/b.

A Poetry Sampler, with an introduction by DH, Franklin Watts, NY, 1962, xxiv, 263 p, h/b.

New Poets of England and America: Second Selection, with Robert Pack, Meridian Books, Cleveland, OH, 1962, 384p, p/b.

Contemporary American Poetry, selected and introduced by DH, Penguin (Penguin Poets series), Baltimore, MD, 1962, 201p, p/b.

Concise Encyclopedia of English and American Poets and Poetry, with Stephen Spender, Hawthorn Books, NY, 1963; Hutchinson, London, 1963, 415p, h/b, with essays by DH on Coventry Patmore, Richard Wilbur, and Poetry and Publishing - United States.

Poetry in English, with Warren Taylor, Macmillan, NY, 1963, 724p, h/b.

A Poetry Sampler, Franklin Watts, NY, 1966, 263p, large print edition.

New Poets of England and America, with Robert Pack and Louis Simpson, and with an introduction by Robert Frost, Meridian Books, NY, 1967, 351p, p/b, second edition.

Man and Boy: an Anthology, Franklin Watts, NY, 1968, 210p, h/b.

The Modern Stylists: Writers on the Art of Writing, The Free Press, NY, 1968, 186p, h/b + p/b.

A Choice of Whitman's Verse, selected, with an Introduction by DH, Faber & Faber, London, 1968, 176p, h/b + p/b.

American Poetry: an Introductory Anthology, Faber & Faber, London, 1969, 192p, h/b + p/b.

Concise Encyclopedia of English and American Poets and Poetry, with Stephen Spender, Hutchinson, London, 1970, 388p, h/b, second edition, revised with new format.

The Harvard Advocate Anthology, Books for Libraries Press, Freeport, NY, 1970, 327p, h/b, second edition.

Poetry in English, with Warren Taylor, Macmillan, NY, 1970, 758p, h/b, second edition.

The Pleasures of Poetry, Harper and Row, NY, 1971, 338p, h/b + p/b.

Contemporary American Poetry, Penguin Books, NY, 1972, 280p, p/b, second edition, revised format.

New Poets of England and America: Second Selection, with Robert Pack, World Publishing Co., NY, 1972, 384p, p/b, second edition.

A Writer's Reader, with D. L. Emblen, Little, Brown, Boston, MA, 1976, 369p, p/b, with Instructor's Manual, 131p, p/b.

Poetry in English, with Warren Taylor, Macmillan, NY, 1978, 758p.

A Writer's Reader, with D. L. Emblen, Little, Brown, Boston, MA, 1979, 500p, p/b, second edition.

To Read Literature, Fiction, Poetry, Drama, Holt, NY, 1981, 1,508p, h/b + p/b.

Oxford Book of American Literary Anecdotes, Oxford University Press, NY, 1981, 360p, h/b + p/b.

To Read Poetry, Holt, NY, 1982, 401p, p/b.

Claims for Poetry, University of Michigan Press, Ann Arbor, MI, 1982, 498p, p/b.

Ploughshares, 8: 2 & 3 (special double issue), 1982, 282p, p/b.

A Writer's Reader, with D. L. Emblen, Little, Brown, Boston, MA, 1982, 504p, p/b, third edition.

To Read Literature, Fiction, Poetry, Drama, Holt, Rinehart and Winston, NY, 1983, 1,258p, p/b, second edition.

The Contemporary Essay, Bedford Books/St. Martin's, NY, 1984, 488p, p/b.

Oxford Book of Children's Verse in America, Oxford University Press, NY, 1985, 319p, h/b; 1990, p/b.

A Writer's Reader, with D.L.Emblen, Foresman, Glenview, IL, 1988, 494p, p/b, fourth edition.

To Read Fiction, Holt, Rinehart and Winston, NY, 1987, 687p, p/b.

To Read Literature, Fiction, Poetry, Drama, Holt, NY, 1987, 1,281p, p/b, third edition.

A Writer's Reader, with D.L.Emblen, Scott, Foresman, Glenview, IL, 1988, 511p, p/b, fifth edition.

New Voices: University and College Poetry Prizes, 1984-1988, The Academy of American Poets, NY, 1989, 135p, p/b.

Best American Poetry 1989, Macmillan, NY, 1989, 293p, p/b; Scribner, NY, h/b.

The Contemporary Essay, St. Martin's Press, NY, 1989, 600p, p/b, second edition.

Anecdotes of Modern Art: from Rousseau to Warhol, with Pat Corrington Wykes, Oxford University Press, NY, 1990, 377p, h/b.

A Writer's Reader, with D. L. Emblen, HarperCollins, NY, 1991, 562p, p/b, sixth edition.

American Poetry: an Introductory Anthology, Faber & Faber, London, 1991, 192p, p/b, second edition.

To Read a Poem, Harcourt, Brace, Jovanovich, Fort Worth, TX, 1992, 411p, p/b, second edition, revised.

To Read Literature, Fiction, Poetry, Drama, Harcourt, Brace College Publishers, Fort Worth, TX, 1992, 1340p, p/b, third edition, revised.

A Writer's Reader, with D. L. Emblen, HarperCollins College Publishers, NY, 1994, 616p, p/b, seventh edition.

The Contemporary Essay, Bedford Books of St. Martin's Press, Boston, MA, 1995, 622p, p/b, third edition.

A Writer's Reader, with D. L. Emblen, Longman, NY, 1997, 655p, p/b, eighth edition.

The Oxford Illustrated Book of American Children's Poems, OUP, NY, 1999, 96p, h/b.

DH WAS THE FOUNDING GENERAL EDITOR OF THE UNDER DISCUSSION SERIES OF BOOKS PUBLISHED BY THE UNIVERSITY OF MICHIGAN PRESS IN ANN ARBOR, MI. LISTED BELOW ARE THE TITLES, EDITORS AND DATES OF PUBLICATION.

Elizabeth Bishop and Her Art, ed. Lloyd Schwartz, 1983.

Richard Wilbur's Creation, ed. Wendy Salinger, 1983.

Reading Adrienne Rich: Reviews and Re-visions, 1951 - 81, ed. Jane R. Cooper, 1984.

On the Poetry of Allen Ginsberg, ed. Lewis Hyde, 1984.

Robert Bly: When Sleepers Awake, ed. Joyce Peseroff, 1984.

Robert Creeley's Life and Work: a Sense of Increment, ed. John Wilson, 1988.
On the Poetry of Galway Kinnell: the Wages of Dying, ed. Howard Nelson, 1988.
On Louis Simpson: Depths Beyond Happiness, ed. Hank Lazer, 1988.
Anne Sexton: Telling the Tale, ed. Steven E. Colburn, 1988.
James Wright: the Heart of the Light, ed. Peter Stitt, 1990.
Frank O'Hara: To Be True to a City, ed. Jim Elledge, 1990.
On the Poetry of Philip Levine: Stranger to Nothing, ed. Christopher Buckley, 1990.
Denise Levertov: Selected Criticism, ed. Albert Gelpi, 1993.
The Poetry of W. D. Snodgrass: Everything Human, ed. Stephen H. Haven, 1993.
On William Stafford: the Worth of Local Things, ed. Tom Andrews, 1995.
On Gwendolyn Brooks: Reliant Contemplation, ed. Stephen C. Wright, 1996.

DH WAS THE FOUNDING GENERAL EDITOR OF THE POETS ON POETRY SERIES OF BOOKS
PUBLISHED BY THE UNIVERSITY OF MICHIGAN PRESS, ANN ARBOR, MI.
LISTED BELOW ARE THE TITLES, AUTHORS AND DATES OF PUBLICATION.

Walking Down the Stairs: Selections from Interviews, Galway Kinnell, 1978.
Writing the Australian Crawl: Views on the Writer's Vocation, William Stafford, 1978.
Trying to Explain, Donald Davie, 1979.
To Make a Prairie: Essays on Poets, Poetry, and Country Living, Maxine Kumin, 1979.
Toward a New Poetry, Diane Wakoski, 1980.
Talking All Morning, Robert Bly, 1980.
Pot Shots at Poetry, Robert Francis, 1980.
Open Between Us, David Ignatow, 1980.
Don't Ask, Philip Levine, 1981.
Living Off the Country: Esays on Poetry and Place, John Haines, 1981.
The Old Poetries and the New, Richard Kostelanetz, 1981.
A Company of Poets, Louis Simpson, 1981.
Parti-Colored Blocks for a Quilt, Marge Piercy, 1982.
Collected Prose, James Wright, 1983.
Old Snow Just Melting: Essays and Interviews, Marvin Bell, 1983.
Writing Like a Woman, Alicia Ostriker, 1983.
A Ballet for the Ear: Interviews, Essays, and Reviews, John Logan, 1983.
Effluences: More Selected Essays and Reviews, Hayden Carruth, 1983.
Collected Prose, Robert Hayden, 1984.
Platonic Scripts, Donald Justice, 1984.
A Local Habitation: Essays on Poetry, John Frederick Nims, 1985.
No Evil Star: Selected Essays, Interviews, and Prose, Anne Sexton, 1985.
The Uncertain Certainty: Interviews, Essays, and Notes on Poetry, Charles Simic, 1985.
The Character of the Poet, Louis Simpson, 1986.
You Must Revise Your Life, William Stafford, 1986.
A Concert for the Tenses: Essays on Poetry, Tess Gallagher, 1986.
Reviews and Essays, 1936 - 55, Weldon Kees, 1988.
Halflife: Improvisations and Interviews, 1977 - 87, Charles Wright, 1988.
Curiosities, William Matthews, 1989.
Wonderful Words, Silent Truth: Essays on Poetry and a Memoir, Charles Simic, 1990.
Poetry Beat: Reviewing the Eighties, compiled by Tom Clark, 1990.
Poems are Hard to Read, William Meredith, 1991.
One of the Dangerous Trades : Essays on the Work and Workings of Poetry, Peter Davison, 1991.

Predecessors, et cetera: Essays, Amy Clampitt, 1991.
Working Time, Jane Miller, 1992.
The Line Forms Here, David Lehman, 1992.
Suicides and Jazzers, Hayden Carruth, 1992.
Words to Create a World: Interviews, Essays, and Reviews of Contemporary Poetry, Daniel
   Hoffman, 1993.
Richer Entanglements, Gregory Orr, 1993.
Plow Naked: Selected Writings on Poetry, Fred Chappell, 1993.
Tales Out of School: Selected Interviews, Robert Creeley, 1993.
Shelf Life: Essays, Memoirs, and an Interview, Thom Gunn, 1993.
The Unemployed Fortune-Teller: Essays and Memoirs, Charles Simic, 1994.
Ships Going Into the Blue: Essays and Notes on Poetry, Louis Simpson, 1994.
The Judge is Fury: Dislocation and Form in Poetry, Mary Kinzie, 1994.
Eloquence and Mere Life: Essays on the Art of Poetry, Alan Williamson, 1994.
Poetry's Old Air, Marianne Boruch, 1995.
The Big Question, David Lehman, 1995.
Robert Lowell's Life and Work: Damaged Grandeur, Richard Tillinghast, 1995.
Trying to Say It: Outlooks and Insights on How Poems Happen, Philip Booth, 1996.

MUSICAL SETTINGS

Three Donald Hall Songs, settings of 'Horse song', 'O Cheese', and 'Wheel of the Ox-Cart',
   for voice and piano, by William Bolcom, E. B. Marks Music Corp., NY, 1979(?), 1
   score, 20p.
Gold, for String Orchestra: after the Poem by Donald Hall, from *Poem Symphonies* by Don
   Freund, MMB Music, St Louis, MO, 199?, 1 score, 10p.
Simple Stories, settings of 'Dancers' and 'Wheel of the oxcart', for soprano solo and chorus
   (SATB) and for chorus (SATB) and flute, clarinet, horn, violoncello, and piano,
   respectively, by William Bolcom, Marks Music, NY, 1991?, 1 score, 26p.
In the Country of Baseball: High Voice and Piano, by David Evan Thomas, based on writings
   by Donald Hall, David Evan Thomas, Minneapolis, MN, 1998, 1 score, 28p.

RECORDINGS

DISCS, AUDIOTAPES & CDS

Poetry Reading, with Geoffrey Hill, Isis Studios, Oxford, UK, 1953, 1 sound disc, 10 min-
   utes.
Donald Hall Reading his Poetry: Selections from Exiles and Marriages, Trans Radio Record-
   ings, Boston, MA, 1955, 1 sound disc, on deposit at the Woodberry Poetry Room,
   Harvard University, Cambridge, MA.
Poetry Reading, 1955, 1 sound tape reel, on deposit at the Woodberry Poetry Room, Harvard
   University, Cambridge, MA, 52 minutes.
Poetry Reading, with Robert Pack, Telavix, Boston, MA, 1956?, 1 sound disc, on deposit at
   the Woodberry Poetry Room, Harvard University, Cambridge, MA, also available

on cassette, 17 minutes.

Poetry Reading, with Robert Pack, Woodberry Poetry Room, Cambridge, MA, 19??, 1 sound tape reel, on deposit at the Woodberry Poetry Room, Harvard University, Cambridge, MA, also available on cassette, 17 minutes.

Poetry Reading, introduced by Harry Levin, Fassett Recording Studio, Boston, MA, 1962, 2 sound discs, on deposit at the Woodberry Poetry Room, Harvard University, Cambridge MA.

Poetry Reading, introduced by Harry Levin, Woodberry Poetry Room, Cambridge, MA, 1962, 2 sound tape reels, on deposit at the Woodberry Poetry Room, Harvard University, Cambridge MA.

The Poetry of Donald Hall, Jeffrey Norton, NY, 1964, YM-YWCA Poetry Center, New York City, November 2, 1964, 26 minutes.

Poetry Reading, Fassett Recording Studio, Boston, MA, 1964, 1 sound disc, on deposit at the Woodberry Poetry Room, Harvard University, Cambridge MA.

Poetry Reading, Woodberry Poetry Room, Cambridge, MA, 1964, 1 sound tape reel, on deposit at the Woodberry Poetry Room, Harvard University, Cambridge MA.

A Summer in the Stomach, Donald Hall, Western Michigan University (WMU Aural Press 1004), Kalamazoo, MI, 1 sound disc, 25 minutes.

An Evening's Frost, 2 sound tape reels, Archive of Recorded Poetry and Literature (A University of Michigan Professional Theatre Program Production), recorded on 1.2.66, Coolidge Auditorium, Library of Congress, Washington, D.C.

Twelve Contemporary Poets, 1966 Houston Poetry Festival Poets Reading Selections of Their Own Works, ed. William J. Scannell for the Poetry Festival at the 1966 Annual Convention of the National Council of Teachers of English, Champaign, IL; The National Council of Teachers of English/Pressed for National Council of Teachers of English by RCA Custom Records, 1966, 1 sound disc.

Treasury of John Greenleaf Whittier, with eleven of Whittier's poems selected and read by DH, Spoken Arts (SA 906), New Rochelle, NY, 1966, 1 sound disc, 51 minutes.

Poetry Reading, at WUOM Radio Station, the University of Michigan, Ann Arbor, MI, 8.6.66, 4 sound tape reels, 1966.

Treasury of Henry Wadsworth Longfellow, poems of Longfellow read by DH, introduced by Arthur Luce Klein, Spoken Arts (SA 898), New Rochelle, NY, 1967, 1 sound disc.

Poetry Reading, with William Edgar Stafford, Coolidge Auditorium, Library of Congress, Washington DC., 6.3.67, 1 sound tape reel, 68 minutes.

Today's Poets: Their Poems, Their Voices, ed. Stephen Dunning, Scholastic Records, NY, 1967, 1 sound disc.

Anthology of Nineteenth Century American Poets, Spoken Arts, New Rochelle, NY, 1969, with readings by DH, Kenneth S. Lynn and Alexander Scourby of poems by Longfellow, Holmes, Whittier, James Russell Lowell, Emerson, Poe and Whitman.

Spoken Arts Treasury of 100 Modern American Poets Reading Their Poems, 17, Spoken Arts, New Rochelle, NY, 1969, SA 1056, with readings by DH and others, 1 sound disc, 51 minutes.

The Pleasures of Poetry, selected and read by DH, introduced by Arthur Luce Klein, Spoken Arts (SA 1100), New Rochelle, NY, 1971, 1 sound disc.

Poetry Reading, introduced by George Plimpton, 1 sound tape reel, on deposit at the Woodberry Poetry Room, Harvard University, Cambridge, MA, also available on cassette, 48 minutes.

The Poetry of Donald Hall, McGraw-Hill (McGraw-Hill sound seminars), NY, 197?, recorded at the Poetry Center of New York, 2.11.64, 320 minutes.

The Poetry of Donald Hall, J. Norton ('Modern poets, writers and critics series'), NY, 1974, recorded at the YM - YWCA Poetry Center, New York City, 2.11.64, 26 minutes.

Poetry Reading, 1975, 1 sound tape reel, on deposit at the Woodberry Poetry Room, Harvard University, Cambridge, MA.

Poets Read Their Work: Donald Hall and Jane Kenyon, Educational Communications Center, State University of New York at Stony Brook (Stony Brook Visiting Poets Series, 6), Stony Brook, NY, 1977.

The Poetry of Donald Hall and Fleur Adcock, Poetry Center Production, State University of New York at Stony Brook (British-American Poetry Festival Videotapes), Stony Brook, NY, 1978.

Jerome Rothenberg talks about enthropoetics and reads some American Indian verse with DH, on *Poets Talking*, 1 sound tape reel, broadcast on University of Michigan TV, January 1978.

Larry Fagin talks about his life, his verse, his ideas about teaching poetry, and the interaction between poetry and painting, with Donald Hall, on *Poets Talking*, 1 sound tape reel, broadcast on University of Michigan TV, 19.1.78.

Some Contemporary Ideas of Prosody, Poetry Center Production, State University of New York at Stony Brook (British-American Poetry Festival Videotape), Stony Brook, NY, 1978.

Spoken Arts Treasury of 100 Modern American Poets, 17, Spoken Arts, New Rochelle, NY, 1978, 1 sound disc, 51 minutes.

Interview with Donald Hall, by Robert Louthan, 1978, 2 sound tape reels, on deposit at Woodberry Poetry Room, Harvard University, Cambridge, MA, 103 minutes.

Poetry Reading, 1978, 1 sound tape reel, on deposit at the Woodberry Poetry Room, Harvard University, Cambridge, MA, also available on audiocassette.

Anthology of 19th Century American Poetry, with DH, Alexander Scourby and Kenneth S. Lynn reading poems by Longfellow, Poe, Whittier, Emerson, Whitman, Holmes and James Russell Lowell, Spoken Arts, New Rochelle, NY, 1979.

The Pleasures of Poetry, Spoken Arts, New Rochelle, NY, 1981, with selections read by DH.

Poetry Reading, with Daniel Mark Epstein, with opening remarks by Henri Cole and introductions by Annie Wright, 1983, 2 sound tape reels, on deposit at the Woodberry Poetry Room, Harvard University, Cambridge, MA, 73 minutes.

Names of Horses, Watershed Intermedia (Watershed tapes Signature Series), Washington, DC., 1985, producer/recording engineer, Katherin Mattern, with DH reading 19 of his poems, the first 11 being recorded at Eagle Pond Farm, Danbury, NH on 13.6.85, and the remainder being recorded at the Folger Shakespeare Library in Washington, D.C. on 15.10.85, 54 minutes.

Spoken Arts Treasury of 100 Modern American Poets Reading Their Poems, 17, Spoken Arts, New Rochelle, NY, 1985, 51 minutes.

Donald Hall, American Poetry Archive, San Francisco, CA, 1986, recorded 20.4.86, 54 minutes.

Poetry Reading, with Etheridge Knight, Coolidge Auditorium, Library of Congress, Washington, D.C, 25.2.86, 1 sound tape reel, 60 minutes.

Treasury of Henry Wadsworth Longfellow, with readings by DH, Spoken Arts, New Rochelle, NY, 1987, 54 minutes.

The One Day, 1988, 1 sound tape reel, on deposit at the Woodberry Poetry Room, Harvard University, Cambridge, MA.

Treasury of Henry Wadsworth Longfellow, with poems selected and read by DH, Baker & Taylor Video, 1992.

Poetry Reading, introduced by Stratis Haviaras, 1993, 1 sound tape reel, on deposit at the Woodberry Poetry Room, Harvard University, Cambridge, MA, also available on cassette, 60 minutes.

Jane Kenyon: A Celebration of Her Life and Works, readings and remembrances by DH and others, recorded 26.10.95, University of New Hampshire Library, Durham, N.H.

Jane Kenyon: a Memorial Tribute, introduced by Stratis Haviaras and Elise Paschen, and including readings by DH and others, held 3.5.96 at Emerson Hall, Harvard University, Cambridge, MA, 1 sound tape reel, on deposit at the Woodberry Poetry Room, Harvard University, Cambridge, MA, 84 minutes.

Donald Hall: Prose and Poetry, Audio Bookshelf, Northport, ME, 1997, 3 hours.

First Jane Kenyon Conference: 16 - 18 April 1998, Bellarmine College, Louisville, KY, 1998, approximately 6 hours, with readings and remembrances by DH and others.

Poetry Reading, introduced by Louisa Solano, at Harvard-Yenching Library, Harvard University, Cambridge, MA, April 21, 1998, 1 sound tape reel, on deposit at the Woodberry Poetry Room, Harvard University, Cambridge, MA, 60 minutes.

The New Hampshire Writers' Project Sampler: Ten Years of Literary Performance, 1988 – 1998, New Hampshire Writers' Project, Concord, NH, 1998, 1 CD, 71 minutes.

Poetry Reading, with Charles Simic, Montpelier Room, Library of Congress, Washington, DC., 4.3.99, program introduced by Prosser Gifford, poets introduced by Robert Pinsky, Library of Congress Magnetic Recording Laboratory, Washington DC., 1999, 1 audiocassette, 75 minutes.

Poetry Reading, introduced by Stratis Haviaras, Lamont Library, Harvard University, Cambridge, MA, April 7, 1999, 1 audiocassette, on deposit at the Woodberry Poetry Room, Harvard University, Cambridge, MA, 60 minutes.

FILMS AND VIDEOTAPES

An Interview: Donald Hall, with Gregory FitzGerald and Rodney Parshall, State University College, Brockport, NY, April 1972.

Donald Hall, University of Michigan Film Video Library ('Poets Talking, 2'), Ann Arbor, MI, 1975, 29 minutes.

Poets Read Their Work: Donald Hall and Jane Kenyon, Educational Communications Center, State University of New York at Stony Brook (Stony Brook Visiting Poets Series, 6), Stony Brook, NY, 1977.

The Poetry of Donald Hall and Fleur Adcock, Poetry Center Production, State University of New York at Stony Brook (British-American Poetry Festival Videotapes), Stony Brook, NY, 1978.

Some Contemporary Ideas of Prosody, Poetry Center Production, State University of New York at Stony Brook (British-American Poetry Festival Videotape), Stony Brook, NY, 1978.

Ox Cart Man, Great Plains National Instructional Television Library and WNED-TV (Reading Rainbow, 18), narrated by Lorne Greene, The Library, Lincoln, NE, 1984, 30 minutes.

Ox Cart Man, Live Oak Media, 1987, Ancramdale, NY, 8 minutes.

Donald Hall and Danny L. Rendleman: Readings, University of Michigan, Flint, MI, 15.4.87 (University of Michigan-Flint Visiting Writers series, 1987), 52 minutes.

The One Day: Poetry Reading, Woodberry Poetry Room, Cambridge, MA, 1988, 1 videocassette, on deposit at the Woodberry Poetry Room, Harvard University, Cambridge, MA.

Donald Hall, HarperCollins Publishers, NY, 1990, 1 videocassette, 55 minutes, recording of a reading given at the 92nd St. Y.M.C.A., Manhattan, 25.9.90.

Bookmark, WNET, NY, hosted by Louis Lapham, 30 minutes.

Poetry Reading, introduced by Stratis Haviaras, 1993, on deposit at the Woodberry Poetry

Room, Harvard University, Cambridge, MA, 60 minutes.

Donald Hall and Jane Kenyon: A Life Together, Films for the Humanities, Inc., ('The Moyers Collection'), Princeton, NJ, 1994, first broadcast on PBS, 17.12.93 as 'Bill Moyers' Journal', 56 minutes.

Baseball, Florentine Films production, a film by Ken Burns; produced by Ken Burns and Lynn Novick; written by Geoffrey C. Ward and Ken Burns, including appearances and commentary by DH, Turner Home Entertainment: PBS Home Video, 1994, 9 videocassettes, originally produced as a television program in 1994, 18 hours, 54 minutes.

Walt Whitman, Mystic Fire Video, NY, 1995, with commentary by DH and others, produced for PBS television in 1986, 60 minutes.

Jane Kenyon: a Celebration of Her Life and Works, readings and remembrances by DH and others, recorded 26.10.95, University of New Hampshire Library, Durham, N.H.

Jane Kenyon: a Memorial Tribute, introduced by Stratis Haviaras and Elise Paschen, and includings readings by DH and others, held 3.5.96 at Emerson Hall, Harvard University, Cambridge, MA, on deposit at the Woodberry Poetry Room, Harvard University, Cambridge, MA, 84 minutes.

'Ox Cart Man', Loma Linda University, 1998.

Poetry Reading, introduced by Louisa Solano, recording of a reading held at Harvard-Yenching Library, Harvard University, Cambridge, MA, 21.4.98, on deposit at the Woodberry Poetry Room, Harvard University, Cambridge, MA, 60 minutes.

Poetry Reading, introduced by Stratis Haviaras, Lamont Library, Harvard University, Cambridge, MA, 7.4.99, 1 videocassette, on deposit at the Woodberry Poetry Room, Harvard University, Cambridge, MA, 60 minutes.

SELECTED SECONDARY WORKS

Crunk,'The Work of Donald Hall', *The Fifties,* Third issue, 1959, pp. 32 - 46.

Ralph J. Mills, Jr., 'Donald Hall's Poetry', *The Iowa Review,* 2:1, Winter 1971, pp. 82 - 125.

'Donald Hall Issue', *Tennessee Poetry Journal,* 4:2, Winter 1971.

Focus 101: an Illustrated Biography of 101 Poets of the 60s and 70s, with photographs, text and editing by LaVerne Harrell Clark, Heidelberg Graphics, Chico, CA,1979, 144p, p/b.

Contemporary Authors, 2 ed. Anne Evory, Gale Research Co., Detroit, MI, 1981, pp. 289 - 291.

Contemporary Authors, New Revision Series, 44, ed. Susan M. Trosky, Gale Research Co., Detroit, MI, 1984, pp. 174 - 177.

Contemporary Authors Autobiography Series, 7, ed. Mark Zadrozny, Gale Research Co., Detroit, MI, 1988.

The Day I Was Older: On the Poetry of Donald Hall, ed. Liam Rector, Story Line Press, Santa Cruz, CA, 1989.

Peter Davison, *The Fading Smile: Poets in Boston from Robert Lowell to Sylvia Plath,* Norton, NY, 1994, 1996, pp. 114 - 121.

Joan Fry, 'An Interview with Donald Hall', *Poets and Writers,* 22:5, September/October 1994, pp. 38 - 51.

Bill Moyers, *The Language of Life: A Festival of Poets,* Doubleday, NY, 1995, pp. 142 - 157.

Marian Blue, 'A Conversation with Poets Donald Hall & Jane Kenyon', *AWP Chronicle,* 17:6, May/Summer 1995, pp. 1 - 8.

'Donald Hall', Mara Ilyse Amster, in *Children's Books and Their Creators*, ed. Anita Silvey, Houghton Mifflin, Boston, MA, 1995, pp. 291 - 292.
'Donald Hall', Robert McDowell, in *Contemporary Poets*, sixth edition, ed. Thomas Riggs, St. James Press, NY, 1996, pp. 425 - 427.
Life at Eagle Pond: The Poetry of Jane Kenyon and Donald Hall, website: http://wwwsc.library.unh.edu/specoll/exhibits/kenhall.htm, online exhibit created and maintained, 1996, by William E. Ross, Special Collections, Librarian, University of New Hampshire, Durham, New Hampshire.
The Café Review, 9, 'Special Issue: Donald Hall', summer 1998.

BIBLIOGRAPHIES

Jack Kelleher, *Donald Hall: a Bibliographical Checklist*, with a foreword by Richard Wilbur, and commentary by DH, Warwick Press, Easthampton, MA, 2000.

THE HALL ARCHIVES

DH's papers are held in the Milne Special Collections and Archives, The University Library, University of New Hampshire.

The Critics

'Poet Donald Hall, 27, has not yet unseated the great oldsters, but with his very first book, he has made a solid seat for himself. *Exiles and Marriages* has neither the poetic blaze of Dylan Thomas nor the suppressed smoulder of Robert Frost, but it has its own true tone composed in almost equal parts of intelligence and imagination.'

Time, review of *Exiles and Marriages*, 1955

'My overall impression of Mr Donald Hall's *Exiles and Marriages* is one of a general level of competence so high that it almost obscures the fact that this volume contains an alarmingly high percentage of poetic odd jobs and merely fashionable exercises.'

William Arrowsmith, review of *Exiles and Marriages*, 1956

'The worst poems, perhaps, are those that confirm us in our own commonplaceness ... Donald Hall's poems are very commonplace, but they are so complacent about themselves that they shock us into awareness of their commonplaceness.'

Randall Jarrell, review of *Exiles and Marriages*, 1956

'Donald Hall's first book was the Lamont Poetry Selection for 1955, and was generously praised everywhere. It was a book of great charm and wit, its assurance and amusement always apparent. The present volume in comparison might be thought solemn. It is, rather, a superbly brave attempt not to repeat the triumph of the first book but to try for something even more difficult: a steady and appraising vision which is earned in art as in life only at great cost.'

Anthony Hecht, review of *The Dark Houses*, 1959

'Perhaps the principal achievement of the book is in Hall's use of syllabic blank verse, two techniques by which he produces an effect where the deliberate flatness of a certain type of free verse is combined with the emotional control of regular metre.'

Thom Gunn, review of *The Dark Houses*, 1959

'Each poem is a sequence of more or less simple statements which fall together – like snow – and hint at the contours of feeling beneath. One is at once satisfied and baffled by the bareness of his poems.'

Martin Dodsworth, review of *A Roof of Tiger Lilies*, 1965

'What is exhibited in these poems is not so much the inability to feel, but the diffident, dispassionate man's inaccessibility to experience, to let loose the demons ... Psychologically, these poems do not fulfil themselves; aesthetically, however, I consider them Hall's most impressive achievement. Special, sparse, magnetic, the best of them haunt the mind, moving on a dark tide, like an ice floe down river.'

Robert Mazzocco, review of *A Roof of Tiger Lilies*, 1965

'The language in the poems I like best is so simple it would be boring if the poems were not so usefully informed by obsession.'

William Matthews, review of *The Alligator Bride: Poems New and Selected*, 1971

'I wish I could call Donald Hall's new book blinding in its intensity and insight; I wish I could call it moving or even interesting; on the other hand, I wish I could say that his work has run downhill since he abandoned "Neo-Augustinism" for whatever he is up to now. Alas, Mr Hall has perhaps improved; alas, he has not improved enough to matter.'

Robert Stock, review of *The Yellow Room: Love Poems*, 1971

'Donald Hall's *The Town of Hill* is terrible. Whatever talent or promise there was in Hall's early books has almost entirely given way to a formulaic pandering to the basest kind of popular taste ...'

Roger Dickinson-Brown, review of *The Town of Hill*, 1978

'*Kicking the Leaves* is a magnificent book of poems; its power comes from Hall's uncanny way with words and from his reliance on a rich source of feeling – memories of his own past, legends of his family's past, myths attaching to the animals and the land. These are poems you will return to many times.'

Peter Stitt, review of *Kicking the Leaves*, 1979

'Hall writes with clarity and honesty ... His words are plain and right, his manner casual and alert ... These poems are a celebration, as [Hall] makes clear, of the poet's middle age. They are a stock-taking, a sifting of values. The raw and unsettling evocations of death by violence ... are, it would seem, deliberate encounters with reality to be faced with a naked mind, without religion or philosophy. And, it must be added, without sentimentality or romantic colouring. Hall has purged fear from his pity (a purging that may be the theme that brings these poems into a unity), giving a kind of awe to his solicitude for the fragility and uncertainty of life.'

Guy Davenport, review of *Kicking the Leaves*, 1979

'The predominant tone of the book is of courage and humility before old values. It is the hardest thing to write poems as simple and celebratory as these, full of love and observation of the commonplace.'

John Fuller, review of *Kicking the Leaves*, 1979

'Over the past six years Donald Hall has been editing an ambitious series of uniform books, collectively titled *Poets on Poetry*, that publishes individually the prose of ... living poets. One simple measure of its value is the conjecture that if a similar collection were done sixty years ago of the prose of a comparable generation of earlier poets, our sense of what they thought they were doing would have been considerably accelerated, if not enhanced.'

Richard Kostelanetz, review of *Claims for Poetry*, 1985

'Hall aspires to an unmediated sincerity and intimacy with the reader, but his method is, paradoxically, academic. He applies a series of formulas to theme and language, and in so doing, seems to alienate himself from his experience.'

Vernon Shetley, review of *Kicking the Leaves*, 1979

'What Hall achieves here and elsewhere is a kind of psalm to the passage, as Freud put it, from hysterical misery to ordinary unhappiness.'

David Shapiro, review of *The Happy Man*, 1987

'Donald Hall's eminence as an editor, teacher and critic of verse has had the ironic effect of overshadowing his own poems, an effect enhanced in recent years by his reticence about publishing new work. Hall is an extreme example of the perfectionist poet, one who writes his poems over and over again until sometimes the copious re-draftings add up to as many pages as the manuscript of a novel. In his pursuit of a poetry worthy of eternity, he refuses to settle for near-misses. *The Happy Man* (the first collection of his to appear in eight years) lives up to Hall's own high standard. His eighth collection of poems in 31 years, it marks a major advance for him, particularly in its strategic use of dramatic voices.'

Tom Clark, review of *The Happy Man*, 1986

'In *The Happy Man* ... Donald Hall discovers a range and intensity of voice one could hardly have guessed at from his earliest work. Hall is one of the most professional and committed of American poets, and it is exciting to find dedication to his craft being so richly rewarded.'

Dean Wilson, review of *The Happy Man*, 1987

'Like many of Hall's poems, the poems of *The Happy Man* have generational and regenerational impulses; one must live both through and beyond these generational echoes and reverberations. The spirits and souls and characters here have chosen to stand, as steadfastly as they are able, against the wastes of time. These poems want to insist upon a transcendence (though Hall would prefer, of course, Eckhardt's "repose" as the term to embody

107

that transcendence) over the body's destruction and the world's griefs. There is a determined, at times willed, quality to this insistence – I don't mean *forced*, I mean *chosen* – that makes me feel that though Hall sees the spirit's victory as natural, perhaps as natural as the body's betrayal and the occasional vacuum of human values, he still sees and wishes to honour the fierce courage of his characters, the courage necessary to find belief or, rather, repose. In this way, confronting the seeming "defeat" of mortality, the spirit joins itself to the timelessness of landscape and natural process. To be *of* nature is, in a basic way, to be no longer the *object* of its seemingly destructive (though regenerative) processes.'

David St John, review of *The Happy Man*, 1987

'It took Donald Hall 17 years to write *The One Day* ... which is Whitmanic in a more orthodox sense [than James Schuyler's long poems]: loud, sweeping, multitudinous, an act of the imperial imagination. A sustained and unified work in three parts rather than a conventional collection, it is the poet's present to himself for his 60th birthday in September. I have no hesitation in declaring it a major book – its passion and urgency are rare and remarkable. Basketball players have a word for hot shooting: the man with the hot hand is shooting "unconscious". This seems an apt description of Hall's method and his magic in *The One Day*.'

David Lehman, review of *The One Day*, 1986

'It is a commonplace that a serious poet aspires to write a long poem. Donald Hall's *The One Day* is ambitious in the best sense; it gives us agency, force, intelligence; it is alive with form and figure; it has (in the final part especially) a passional yet thoughtful tone that requires our assent to the whole work. Hall has said that "There is no way to be good except by trying to be great." He has embraced the need the strong poet has to write a long poem and has succeeded impressively. Hall is more than a good poet.'

Stephen Sandy, review of *The One Day*, 1988

'Among his numerous prose books, Hall has written at least one, *Remembering Poets* (1978), which is of permanent value, not only for its observant memoirs of Dylan Thomas, Frost, Eliot, and Pound, but for the brilliant way he moves from them into his reflections about the nature of poetry itself. He says "poetry attempts ... to add old or irrational elements to the light of consciousness by means of language, which is the instrument of consciousness." The poet thus adds unreason to reason, "making a third thing." It seems to me that this describes well what Hall has done in *The One Day*: mere reason was combined with mere irrationality and the two in combination produce the refined and alert awareness, the late spring, of the third part, a life going through the same processes as a poetry.

And this poem, as a whole, may indeed be seen as the synthesis of a whole life's work. It is one of those books, like Elizabeth Bishop's last collection, which alters the way we look at the jumbled contents of the poetic career preceding it, giving it retrospectively a shape, a pattern, a consistency it didn't seem to have at the time.'

Thom Gunn, review of *The One Day*, 1989

'*The One Day* has about it the wicked satire of a Tom Wolfe, an Old Testament razzmatazz of rant, a prophetic energy akin to Allen Ginsberg's *Howl*, and a lyricism which bears Hall's fully developed signature.'

Liam Rector, review of *The One Day*, 1993

'... several times in his career Hall has foundered, has fallen into dry spells and halted verse composition entirely. Then he found a way to begin anew, writing in a style that looks radically different from what came before ...

The broad variety of Hall's writing has long been a source of wonder. Besides poetry and criticism, he has published fiction, drama, children's literature, biography, and reminiscence. His poetry encompasses all sorts of forms, from steely epigrams, like the one addressed to a philosopher ("The world is everything that is the case. / Now stop your blubbering and wash your face"), to an attempt at a contemporary epic. This latter poem, called *The One Day*, is an honourable attempt, but hobbled by muddy organization and some puffy rhetoric. It won an award from the National Book Critics Circle, a group whose selection committees have boasted in the organization's newsletter that they don't like poetry and don't read it.

But it is not Hall's fault that a horde of critical midges have conspired to give him a prize for work that is not his best. His best work is very fine indeed and there is plenty of it. So much of it, in fact, that my list of favourite poems is too long to include here. But I will name a few I consider among the best written in two generations: "Exile", "At Delphi", "The Long River", "The Moon", "Beau of the Dead", "In The Kitchen of the Old House", "The Blue Wing", "The Table", "Kicking the Leaves", "The Black-Faced Sheep", "Names of Horses", "Whip-Poor-Will", "Old Timers' Day" and "On a Horse Carved in Wood".

Knowing readers will see that I've included a few Deep Image poems among my tiptop favourites. When Donald Hall is writing well, he can bring to almost any kind of discourse a profound and polished wit, a fineness of observation that a naturalist might envy, and a warm and ready affection. These qualities are controlled by a firm intelligence, a sly curiosity, and a wary critical sense.'

Fred Chappell, review of *Old and New Poems*, 1991

'Though Hall is in his sixties, his newest work contains the same vim and spark that drives his older poems, approaching the level of achievement realized in what may be the finest, 'Kicking the Leaves'. A fascinating and rewarding omnibus.'

Fred Muratori, review of *Old and New Poems*, 1991

'... few writers could have taken such apparently slight anecdotes of country life and made them, so unobtrusively but surely, into such profoundly authoritative icons of human experience.'

Dick Davis, review of *Old and New Poems*, 1991

'This is poetry that marches in a stately order; classical in its dignity and perfectly readable, it argues the mystical union od dark and light, death and life.'

Review of *Old and New Poems*, *New York Times Book Review*, 1993

'The best new book I have read this year, of extraordinary nobility and wisdom. It will remain with me always.'

Louis Begley, review of *Life Work*, 1993

'A sustained meditation on work as the key to personal happiness ... *Life Work* reads most of all like a first-person psychological novel with a poet named Donald Hall as its protagonist ... Hall's particular talents ultimately [are] for the memoir, a genre in which he has few living equals. In his hands the memoir is only partially an autobiographical genre. He pours both his full critical intelligence and poetic sensibility into the form.'

Dana Gioia, review of *Life Work*, 1993

'Near the beginning of the book Hall expresses the hope that he is doing his "Best Work – although I understand that it is unlikely at sixty-three and a half." Unlikely it may be, but in *The Museum of Clear Ideas* and *Life Work* this is exactly what Donald Hall has done, and we are the beneficiaries.'

William Pritchard, joint review of *The Museum of Clear Ideas* and *Life Work*, 1993

'Donald Hall is our finest elegist. *The Museum of Clear Ideas* is as original, idiosyncratic, and un-museumlike a poetic work as we are likely to see for a long time to come.'

Richard Tillinghast, review of *The Museum of Clear Ideas*, 1993

'The work of a master, all the more poignant for its frankness and unsentimentality in the face of tragedy.'

Pittsburgh Post-Gazette, Review of *The Old Life*, 1996

'These autobiographical poems are free of self-pity, engagingly frank without being in any sense 'confessional', and often wildly comic ... All are first-rate.'

Minneapolis Star-Tribune, Review of *The Old Life,*1996

'A heartbreaking portrait of a marriage that death has not quite ended. Documents of a numb grief ... flashes of despair, lust and gratitude. Hall is unflinching, showing us agonies both physical and mental.'

Publishers' Weekly, review of *Without*, 1998

'An extraordinary collection, honouring the life, and lamenting the death, of his wife and fellow poet, Jane Kenyon.'

Vanity Fair, review of *Without*, 1998

FOR FURTHER INFORMATION, PLEASE CONTACT:

Between The Lines

9 WOODSTOCK ROAD
LONDON N4 3ET
UK

TEL: +44 (0)20 7272 8719
FAX: +44 (0)20 8374 5736

E-MAIL: BETWEENTHELINES@LINEONE.NET

WEBSITE: HTTP//WWW.INTERVIEWS-WITH-POETS.COM